Commemorative History

TURNER PUBLISHING COMPANY
Nashville, Tennessee

Publisher's of America's History

www.turnerpublishing.com

Copyright © 2004 Turner Publishing Company
All rights reserved.

Turner Publishing Staff:
Editor: Eddie Sheridan
Designer: Ina F. Morse

This book or any part thereof may not be reproduced without the express written consent of the publisher. This publication was complied using available and submitted materials. The publisher regrets it cannot assume liability for errors or omissions.

The 9th Air Force/United States Central Command Air Forces (USCENTAF) emblem appears with permission from the Department of Air Force/United States Central Command Air Forces. The 9th Air Force Association and its activities are not officially endorsed or supported by the 9th AF/USCENTAF.

Library of Congress Catalog No. 2003117132

ISBN: 978-1-68162-286-6

"ALL GAVE SOME — SOME GAVE ALL"

"Marauder Mission" by Robert Taylor. B-26 Marauders of the 386th Bomb Group, 9th Air Force, returning from a strike against the V.I. rocket sites in the Pas de Calais, January 1944. (Courtesy of Lloyd Johnson)

TABLE OF CONTENTS

Foreword 6
Preface 7
History 8
Airfields in Europe on which Ninth Air Force Units were based 24
The Engineer Aviation Regiments and Battalions 26
Special Stories 28
Biographies 48
Photo Album 99
Index 104

Foreword

Colonel Raymond P. Lowman

The Ninth Air Force Association, in conjunction with Turner Publishing Company, is privileged to bring you this Ninth Air Force History Book. There have been some challenges and delays, but these have been overcome, resulting in a proud record of the monumental accomplishments of those assigned to the Ninth Air Force. Two of the purposes for the which The Ninth Air Force Association exists is: (1) To preserve and publicize the history of the Ninth Air Force from its beginning in World War II to the present and (2) To honor and memorialize the sacrifices of our comrades and families. I think you will agree that these pages do just that.

The Ninth Air Force became operational in November 1942. Its air support of the British and United States armies in Africa against the Nazis' Rommel was critical. By June 6, 1944, D-Day, it had become the largest Air Force ever assembled under one command. It consisted of Fighter, Bomber, Troop Carrier, Air Defense, Engineer, and Service Commands. Since World War II, the Ninth Air Force has continued its role of providing combat-ready, proficient air power. For all Ninth Air Force veterans, it is more than reasonable to reflect back and realize that the Ninth has been a foremost determining factor in all major U.S. military actions during the past 60-plus years.

A word about The Ninth Air Force Association: The Association began on July 20, 1990, when representatives from nine World War II units gathered in St. Louis, Missouri. Talks focused on the meager public knowledge of the illustrious history of the Ninth AF, and it was agreed this Association should be established to perform this service. Those founding members should be recognized, and they are: Leonard Bennett, Harold Crocker, Martin Engler, Fred Fehsenfeld, Laurence C. Gaughran, George Johnson, Lloyd Johnson, Edward F. MacLean, Charles F. Mann, Fred Munder, John Peterson, Marvin J. Rosvold, George Wagasky Jr., and John B. Yarger. We are indebted to them for the many accomplishments of The Ninth Air Force Association, including this book. Your Association serves as an umbrella organization for all units ever assigned to The Ninth Air Force. All are invited and encouraged to participate (individually or by unit) in our annual conventions and other special activities.

I sincerely hope you enjoy reading and take pride in ownership of this document reflecting the sacrifices and accomplishments of many heroes.

Raymond P. Lowman

Colonel Raymond P. Lowman
USAF (Ret.)
Chairman, Board of Directors
The Ninth Air Force Association

PREFACE

Lt. Colonel Stanley E. Stepnitz

In June of 1942, General Rommel was having a lot of success against the English. Under the command of General Brereton, air power in the form of B-17s he had brought from India and B-24 aircraft Colonel Halverson had been ferrying toward China proved very useful for the British armies. In addition to the bombers, Colonel Mears launched a group of P-40 fighter aircraft from the aircraft carrier "Ranger" and joined the bombers in the fight against the German army.

This successful use of air power by what was at that time the Middle East Air Force proved the value of such a combination of aircraft. On 12 November 1942, the MEAF was redesignated the Ninth Air Force with General Brereton as Commander. Under his command, the force began to expand in numbers and strength. More fighters and bombers were acquired, as well as the addition of troop carrier aircraft. With this added muscle, the Ninth moved into battle in Italy and then in Sicily.

Next, it was time to move into position for the invasion of France. The Ninth was then moved to England in October 1943. As attacks on Nazi positions throughout Europe increased in intensity, the size of the Ninth continued to grow in value and strength to become the largest tactical Air Force ever assembled. When D-Day came, the Ninth was ready with fighters, bombers, and troop carriers to lead the way to victory.

After World War II, the Ninth Air Force came home to the United States and remained ready and capable to perform duty wherever needed. The Headquarters is now located at Shaw AFB, South Carolina. Elements of this remarkable organization are located at several locations in the eastern United States. Always a force to be reckoned with, by gaining air superiority over any foe, by destroying the capability of any enemy to replenish supplies and to provide close support to ground forces.

All past and present members of the Ninth Air Force can hold their heads high. They have a heritage for which they can be proud.

Stanley E. Stepnitz
Lt. Col., USAF (Ret.)
President

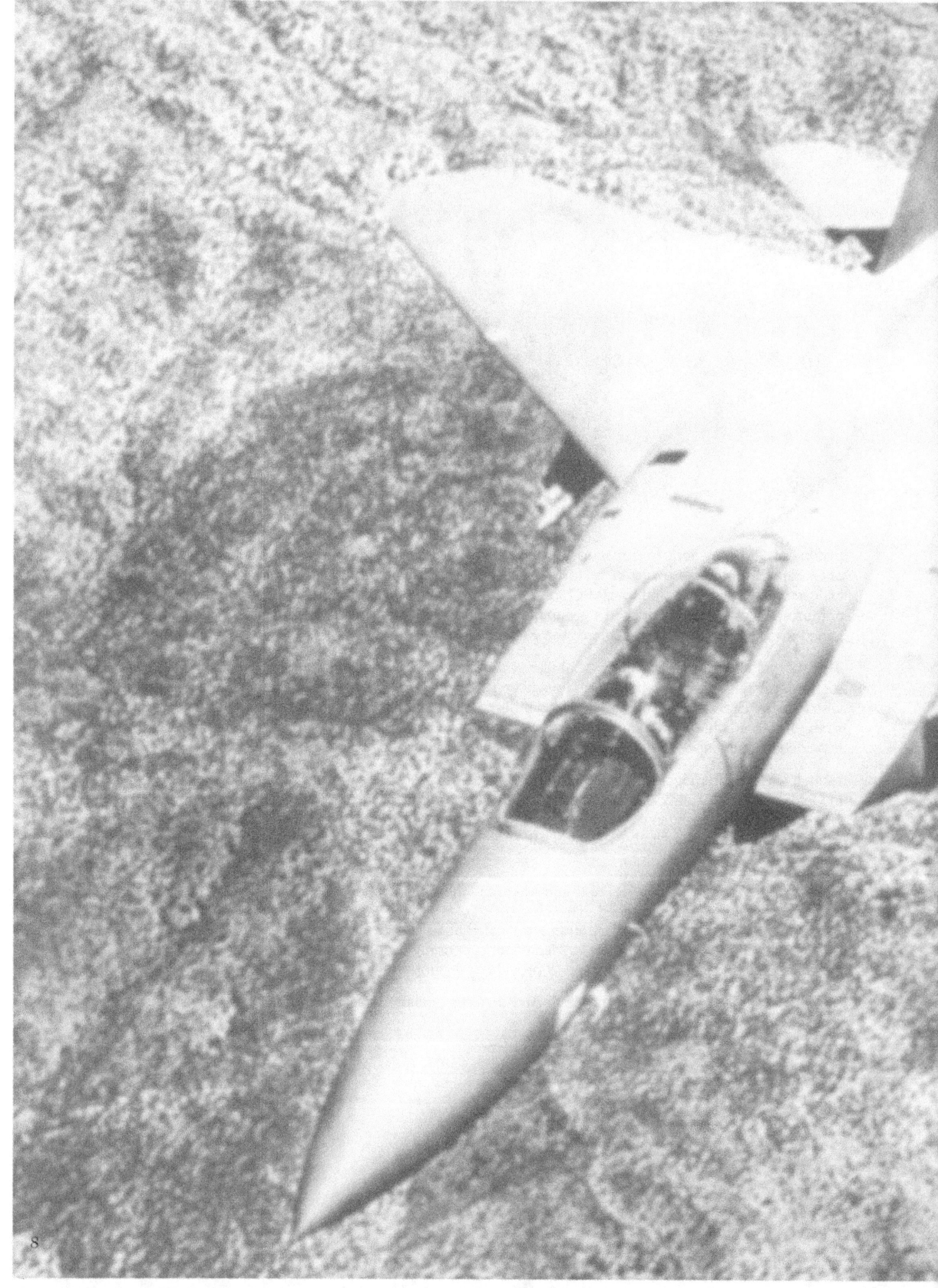

Ninth Air Force History

90th Troop Carrier SQ./438th Troop Carrier Group. C-47 towing CG-4A Glider.

389th Fighter SQ./366th Fighter Group. P-47.

Nine Battle Stars:
Men of the Ninth Air Force

Prepared by
Michael N. Ingrisano, Jr.

Background:

At its maximum in World War II, the United States Army Air Force (USAAF) numbered more than 2,400,000 men and women. There were power and glider pilots, navigators, bombardiers, gunners, crew chiefs (flight engineers), radio operators, clerks and typists, artists, teachers, aircraft, glider and vehicle mechanics, and vehicle drivers, statisticians, and mechanical engineers. All skills necessary to conduct and support the air war. From privates to generals, they all had to be molded into organizations capable of supplying direction and coordination of these diverse activities.

In the organizational scale for combat, these entities were formed upward into numbered squadrons, groups, wings, commands, and into 16 air forces in the USAAF. The Ninth Air Force was among the latter designations.

In January 1939, President Franklin D. Roosevelt asked the Congress to strengthen America's then inadequate air power. In September 1939, when Adolph Hitler of Nazi Germany attacked Poland, the second World War began. As the Axis (Germany and Italy) forces gained victory after victory, the United States Army's air arm grew so that by the end of 1940, it had 30 groups, up from its 1939 level of 15. By the time that Japan attacked Pearl Harbor on 7 December 1941, and the United States entered the war, the number of active groups had increased to 67. Many were still being organized and few had suitable combat aircraft.

By the end of 1943, there were 269 groups. Through mission refinements and reorganizations, the number dropped to 218 combat groups. By February 1945, the number of combat groups had risen to 243. With the invasion of Europe in June 1944, and the continuing campaigns in Italy, the United States had 148 combat groups in the European-African-Middle Eastern Theater (EAMET). The Ninth, along with the Eighth, Twelfth, and Fifteenth Air Forces operated in this theater.

The Ninth Air Force:

The Ninth Air Force was initially constituted as the V Air Support Command on 21 August 1941. Under the command of Brigadier General Junius W. Jones, it was activated in Bowman Field, Kentucky, on 1 September 1941. In January 1942, under the

442nd Night Fighter SQ. P-61 Black Widow.

command of Colonel Rosenham Beam, it was moved to the New Orleans, Louisiana, Army Air Force Base, where in April 1942 it was redesignated Ninth Air Force. In July 1942, it was moved to Bolling Field in Washington, D.C., and remained there until October 1942.

439th TCG. C-47s loading 82nd Airborne for Holland.

In the Middle East and Africa: Under the command of Lt. General Lewis H. Brereton, the Ninth left the United States for Egypt and began operations on 12 November 1942. There, the Ninth Air Force, with the support of its newly designated IX Fighter Command, and the 316th Troop Carrier Groups (later to be incorporated into the IX Troop Carrier Command) participated in the Allied drive across Egypt and Libya, and in the campaign in Tunisia. The Ninth completed its missions in the Africa-Middle East Theater when, with the support of the growing IX Troop Carrier Command, it dropped the 82nd Airborne Division into Sicily on July 9-12, 1943, in Operations Husky 1 and 2, and into Italy in September 1943, for the Giant Operations.

England and the European Theater: On 16 October 1943, the Ninth, still under the command of General Brereton, moved its headquarters to Sunninghill Park, England, in preparation for the aerial assault on Normandy, France. It was during this period that the Ninth Air Force rounded out its organization to include the following components: IX Fighter Command (1942-1945); IX Tactical Air Command (1943-1944); IX Bomber Command (formerly 9th Air Division — 1942-1944); the IX Troop Carrier Command (1943-1944); and support units, the IX Air Defense Command and the IX Aviation Engineers. Its combined mission was the bombing and strafing of strategic targets over the coast of and into the interior of France and throughout the campaign in Europe. The Troop Carrier Command led the U.S. vertical assault on Normandy by dropping paratroopers and glider infantry and artillerymen of the 82nd and 101st Airborne Divisions, and flying resupply and evacuation support missions into Normandy.

On 8 August 1944, General Dwight D. Eisenhower appointed General Brereton commander of the First Allied Airborne Army (FAAA). Under his successor,

General Hoyt S. Vanderburg, the structure of the Ninth Air Force changed to: IX Air Defense Command (1944-1945), the XIX Tactical Air Command (1944-1945 — formerly XIX Air Support Command), and the XIX Tactical Air Command (1945).

The IX Troop Carrier Command became a part of the FAAA and participated in the vertical assault of Holland in Operation Market Garden, 17-26 September 1944. Its components again dropped paratroopers, towed glider infantry and artillerymen, and landed supplies for the 82nd and 101st Airborne Divisions.

As the Allied armies moved across France and finally into Germany, the Ninth also moved on to bases in these countries. The tactical air and bomb commands continued operations from these bases, supporting ground force until the end of the war. The Troop Carrier Command flew its final combat mission on 24 March 1945 in Operation Varsity. In this operation, the command dropped paratroopers of the British 6th Airborne Division and of the U.S. 17th Airborne Division, and also towed in elements of the 17th in this vertical assault over the Rhine River into Germany.

355th FSQ/354 FG. P-51B.

451st Bomb SQ./322 Bomb Group. B-26.

71st TCS/434 TCG. C-47.

Although World War II ended in August 1945, the Ninth Air Force was not to leave Germany for the United States (Zone of the Interior) until December 1945. There it was shifted to various bases until 20 August 1954, when it was stationed permanently at Shaw Air Force Base, South Carolina.

Components of the Ninth Air Force in World War II

The primary source for the history of the Ninth in WWII is *Air Force Combat Units of World War II*, edited by Maurer Maurer, originally published by the U.S. Government Office, Washington, D.C., 1961.

This reference book is structured so that a researcher can derive the details of each air combat unit that served in WWII. The chapters follow organizations upward: Groups, Wings, Divisions, Commands, Air Forces. In each of those major headings are listings of the various components in a combat unit. (For example, under the heading of HQ.IX Tactical Air Command, we find the 70th Fighter Wing, 48th Fighter Group which was organized into the 492nd, 493rd, and 494th Fighter Squadrons, primarily flying P-47 Thunderbolts.)

Any attempt to trace each of these components through its ascendancy would not only be a tedious task, but would be tiresome for the reader.

The Ninth Air Force Units in England: The study by Roger A. Freeman, *UK AIRFIELDS OF THE NINTH THEN AND NOW*, London: Battle of Brittain Prints International Limited, 1994, provides a recapitulation of pertinent data for each unit.

In his heavily illustrated book, Freeman does an analysis comparable to what is found in Maurer's book. For the air fields used by the Ninth in England, he details the architectural history of each field, its occupants during WWII, and into its post-war fate. Some of the fields are still active, but, by and large, most are memories for the men and women who served in a particular locale.

Fortunately, to save the reader the task of reading the fine print, Freeman, in his introduction, has condensed much of the Ninth Air Force's component history into several very informative charts. These are included with the kind permission of the original author.

Chart 1: Plan for the Disposition of Ninth Air Force Units, October 1943

This chart provides insight into the Ninth's planning phase of pulling together the combat units into a controlled area as it readied itself for the Allied invasion of Europe. It does not define specific components, but it does provide a general organizational label, such as: Fighter Group, Bomb Group, Troop Carrier Group, and the proposed base in England for that type of aircraft and its mission.

107th Tac Recon SQ./67th Tac Recon GP. P-6C [P-51C]

PLAN FOR THE DISPOSITION OF NINTH AIR FORCE UNITS, OCTOBER 1943

Type of Unit	Winter Location	Expected date of occupation	Tactical Disposition Spring 1944	Type of Unit	Winter Location	Expected date of occupation	Tactical Disposition Spring 1944
Ninth AF HQ	Sunninghill Park	Occupied	Uxbridge — Tactical Sunninghill — Admin	Bomb Group	Earls Colne	Occupied	Same
				Bomb Group	Gosfield	3/44	Same
Tac Recon Group	Middle Wallop	11/43	Same	HQ Bomb Wing (Medium)	Chipping Ongar	Occupied	Same
Photo Recon Group	Chalgrove	1/44	Same	Bomb Group	Chipping Ongar	Occupied	Same
				Bomb Group	Boreham	4/44	Same
				Bomb Group	Matching	1/44	Same
HQ IX Fighter Command	Middle Wallop	11/43	Uxbridge — Command	HQ Bomb Wing	Great Dunmow	Occupied	Same
HQ Fighter Division	Aldermaston Court	11/43	Middle Wallop	Bomb Group	Great Dunmow	Occupied	Same
				Bomb Group	Andrews Field	Occupied	Same
				Bomb Group	Stansted	2/44	Same
HQ Fighter Wing	Boxted	11/43	Ibsley	HQ IX Troop Carrier Command	Grantham Lodge	12/43	Same
Fighter Group	Boxted	11/43	Stoney Cross	HQ Troop Carrier Wing	Bottesford	Occupied	Same
Fighter Group	Wormingford	11/43	Tarrant Rushton				
Fighter Group	Raydon	11/43	Warmwell	Troop Carrier Group	Fullbeck	Occupied	Same
Fighter Group	Rivenhall	12/43	Bisterne				
Fighter Group	Birch	12/43	Ibsley	Troop Carrier Group	Langar	11/43	Same
HQ Fighter Wing	Ibsley	1/44	Beaulieu	Troop Carrier Group	Mullaghmore	12/43	Leicester East
Fighter Group	Holmsley South	1/44	Lymington	Troop Carrier Group	Balderton	12/43	Same
Fighter Group	Warmwell	2/44	Winkton				
Fighter Group	Ibsley	3/44	Beaulieu	Troop Carrier Group	Bottesford	1/44	Same
Fighter Group	Tarrant Rushton	4/44	Christchurch				
Fighter Group	Stoney Cross	5/44	Zeals	HQ Troop Carrier Wing	Cottesmore	Occupied	Same
HQ Fighter Wing	Greenham Common	12/43	Andover	Troop Carrier Group	Barkston Heath	1/44	Same
Fighter Group	Membury	12/43	Andover	Troop Carrier Group	Folkingham	4/44	Same
Fighter Group	Greenham Common	12/43	Chilbolton				
Fighter Group	Aldermaston	1/44	Thruxton	Troop Carrier Group	Cottesmore	2/44	Same
HQ Fighter Division	Rudloe	2/44	Biggin Hill	Troop Carrier Group	Saltby	4/44	Same
HQ Fighter Wing	Keevil	2/44	Lashenden	HQ Troop Carrier Wing	North Luffenham	3/44	Same
Fighter Group	Keevil	2/44	Lashenden	Troop Carrier Group	North Luffenham	3/44	Same
Fighter Group	Zeals	3/44	Headcorn				
Fighter Group	Weston Zoyland	4/44	Staplehurst	Troop Carrier Group	Wakerley	3/44	Same
Fighter Group	Merryfield	3/44	High Halden	Troop Carrier Group	Woolfox Lodge	3/44	Same
HQ Fighter Wing	Exeter	3/44	Ashford				
Fighter Group	Exeter	3/44	Ashford	Troop Carrier Group	North Witham	3/44	Same
Fighter Group	Upottery	3/44	Woodchurch				
Fighter Group	Church Stanton	3/44	Brenzett	HQ Ninth AF Service Command	Sunninghill Park	12/43	Same
Fighter Group	Winkleigh	4/44	Kingsnorth	Advanced Air Depot	Stansted	Occupied	Same
Night Fighter Group	Charmy Down	2/44	Same	Advanced Air Depot	Grove	Occupied	Same
HQ Bomb Wing (Light)	Blakehill Farm	1/44	Undecided	Advanced Air Depot	Membury	12/43	Same
Bomb Group(L)	Blakehill Farm	1/44	Undecided				
Bomb Group(L)	Down Ampney	2/44	Undecided	Advanced Air Depot	Bottesford	12/43	Same
Bomb Group(L)	Fairford	3/44	Undecided				
HQ IX Bomber Command	Marks Hall	Occupied	Same	Advanced Air Depot	Undecided	?	Undecided
HQ Bomb Wing (Medium)	Earls Colne	Occupied	Same				

In August 1943, the Eighth Air Force was notified that it was to be allocated a total 115 combat groups, the last to reach the UK in the spring of 1944. Although such schedules fluctuated from month to month, it appeared there would be difficulty in finding sufficient airfields in southern and eastern England to base this enormous force. The strategic element consisted of 54 heavy bomber groups, 15 fighter groups, and a reconnaissance group. The tactical assignment was 11 medium and light bomber groups, 20 fighter-bomber, five reconnaissance, and nine-and-a-half troop carrier groups. The following month, the situation was alleviated by the decision to divert 14 new heavy bomber groups to Italy and form the Fifteenth Air Force. USAAF high command also decided to transfer the tactical mission of the Eighth Air Force to the Ninth Air Force, transferred from the Mediterranean to the UK, although this was basically a re-designation of existing tactical headquarters. In late October 1943, the Ninth Air Force issued its plan for the disposition of its units as advised at that time. As many fighter-bomber groups would eventually have to operate from temporary landing ground that were unsuitable for winter occupation, and several other airfields provided by the British were not yet available or required additional work before a whole U.S. fighter group could be accommodated, a programme for winter quarters was set up. Many groups arrived much later than scheduled and, in the event, there was no need to use several of the winter dispositions. The groups of the 84th Fighter Wing planned for the Exeter area were placed on advanced landing grounds in Kent as soon as they reached the UK.

Chart 2: U.S. Ninth Air Force in the United Kingdom; Combat Units with Locations and Principal Aircraft Types

The caption tells most of the story, but Freeman also includes the smallest component, the squadron. And by including the location, he has provided each veteran who served in the Ninth Air Force an indelible physical memory of life in the United Kingdom.

U.S. NINTH AIR FORCE IN THE UNITED KINGDOM
COMBAT UNITS WITH LOCATIONS AND PRINCIPAL AIRCRAFT TYPE

HQ NINTH AIR FORCE
SUNNINGHILL PARK, ASCOT

HQ IX FIGHTER COMMAND
MIDDLE WALLOP

422nd Night Fighter Squadron
Charmy Down, Scorton
P-61 Black Widow

425th Night Fighter Squadron
Charmy Down, Scorton
P-61 Black Widow

HQ IX TACTICAL AIR COMMAND
ALDERMASTON COURT, MIDDLE WALLOP, UXBRIDGE

67th Tactical Reconnaissance Group
12th TRS, 15th TRS, 107th TRS, 109th TRS, 153rd LS,
30th PRS, 9th WRS(P)
Membury, Middle Wallop
F-6 Mustang, F-5 Lightning

368th Fighter Group
395th FS, 396th FS, 397th FS
Greenham Common, Chilbolton
P-47 Thunderbolt

70th FIGHTER WING
Greenham Common, Boxted, Ibsley

370th Fighter Group
401st FS, 402nd FS, 485th FS
Andover
P-38 Lightning

48th Fighter Group
492nd FS, 493rd FS, 494th FS
Ibsley
P-47 Thunderbolt

367th Fighter Group
392nd FS, 393rd FS, 394th FS
Stoney Cross, Ibsley
P-38 Lightning

84TH FIGHTER WING
Keevil, Beaulieu

50th Fighter Group
10th FS, 81st FS, 313th FS
Lymington
P-47 Thunderbolt

371st Fighter Group
404th FS, 405th FS, 406th FS
Bisterne
P-47 Thunderbolt

365th Fighter Group
386th FS, 387th FS, 388th FS
Gosfield, Beaulieu
P-47 Thunderbolt

474th Fighter Group
428th FS, 429th FS, 430th FS
Warmwell
P-38 Lightning

404th Fighter Group
506th FS, 507th FS, 508th FS
Winkton
P-47 Thunderbolt

71ST FIGHTER WING
Aldermaston, Greenham Common

405th Fighter Group
509th FS, 510th FS, 511th FS
Christchurch
P-47 Thunderbolt

366th Fighter Group
389th FS, 390th FS, 391st FS
Andover, Membury, Thruxton
P-47 Thunderbolt

HQ XIX TACTICAL AIR COMMAND
MIDDLE WALLOP, ALDERMASTON COURT

363rd Fighter Group
380th FS, 381st FS, 382nd FS
Keevil, Rivenhall, Staplehurst
P-51 Mustang

10th Photo Reconnaissance Group
30th PRS, 31st PRS, 33rd PRS, 34th PRS, 155th NPS, 15th TRS
Chalgrove
F-5 Lightning, F-6 Mustang, A-20 Havoc

303RD FIGHTER WING
Ashford

100TH FIGHTER WING
Boxted, Greenham Common, Ibsley, Lashenden

36th Fighter Group
22nd FS, 23rd FS, 53rd FS
Kingsnorth
P-47 Thunderbolt

354th Fighter Group
353rd FS, 355th FS, 356th FS
Greenham Common, Boxted, Lashenden
P-51 Mustang

373rd Fighter Group
410th FS, 411th FS, 412th FS
Woodchurch
P-47 Thunderbolt

358th Fighter Group
365th FS, 366th FS, 367th FS
Raydon, High Halden
P-47 Thunderbolt

406th Fighter Group
512th FS, 513th FS, 514th FS
Ashford
P-47 Thunderbolt

362nd Fighter Group
377th FS, 378th FS, 379th FS
Wormingford, Headcorn
P-47 Thunderbolt

IX BOMBER COMMAND
MARKS HALL

97TH COMBAT BOMB WING
Marks Hall, Little Walden

409th Bomb Group
640th BS, 641st BS, 642nd BS, 643rd BS
Little Walden
A-20 Havoc

410th Bomb Group
644th BS, 645th BS, 646th BS, 647th BS
Birch, Gosfield
A-20 Havoc

416th Bomb Group
668th BS, 669th BS, 670th BS, 671st BS
Wethersfield
A-20 Havoc

98TH COMBAT BOMB WING
Earls Colne, Beaulieu

323rd Bomb Group
453rd BS, 454th BS, 455th BS, 456th BS
Earls Colne, Beaulieu
B-26 Marauder

387th Bomb Group
556th BS, 557th BS, 558th BS, 559th BS
Chipping Ongar, Stoney Cross
B-26 Marauder

394th Bomb Group
584th BS, 585th BS, 586th BS, 587th BS
Boreham, Holmesley South
B-26 Marauder

397th Bomb Group
596th BS, 597th BS, 598th BS, 599th BS
Gosfield, Rivenhall, Hurn
B-26 Marauder

99TH COMBAT BOMB WING
Great Dunmow

1st Pathfinder Squadron (P)
Andrews Field
B-26 Marauder

322nd Bomb Group
449th BS, 450th BS, 451st BS, 452nd BS
Andrews Field
B-26 Marauder

344th Bomb Group
494th BS, 495th BS, 496th BS, 497th BS
Stansted
26 Marauder

386th Bomb Group
552nd BS, 553rd BS, 554th BS, 555th BS
Great Dunmow
B-26 Marauder, A-26 Invader

391st Bomb Group
572nd BS, 573rd BS, 574th BS, 575th BS
Matching
B-26 Marauder

IX TROOP CARRIER COMMAND
COTTESMORE, GRANTHAM, ASCOT

IX TCC Pathfinder Group (P)
1st PFS(P), 2nd PFS(P), 3rd PFS(P), 4th PFS(P)
North Witham, Chalgrove
C-47 Skytrain

50TH TROOP CARRIER WING
Cottesmore, Bottesford, Exeter

439th Troop Carrier Group
91st TCS, 92nd TCS, 93rd TCS, 94th TCS
Balderton, Upottery
C-47 Skytrain

440th Troop Carrier Group
95th TCS, 96th TCS, 97th TCS, 98th TCS
Bottesford, Exeter
C-47 Skytrain

441st Troop Carrier Group
99th TCS, 100th TCS, 301st TCS, 302nd TCS
Langar, Merryfield
C-47 Skytrain

442nd Troop Carrier Group
303rd TCS, 304th TCS, 305th TCS, 306th TCS
Fulbeck, Weston Zoyland
C-47 Skytrain

52ND TROOP CARRIER WING
Cottesmore

61st Troop Carrier Group
14th TCS, 15th TCS, 53rd TCS, 59th TCS
Barkston Heath
C-47 Skytrain

313th Troop Carrier Group
29th TCS, 47th TCS, 48th TCS, 49th TCS
Folkingham
C-46 Commando, C-47 Skytrain

314th Troop Carrier Group
32nd TCS, 50th TCS, 61st TCS, 62nd TCS
Saltby
C-47 Skytrain

315th Troop Carrier Group
34th TCS, 43rd TCS, 309th TCS, 310th TCS
Aldermaston, Welford, Spanhoe
C-47 Skytrain

316th Troop Carrier Group
36th TCS, 37th TCS, 44th TCS, 45th TCS
Cottesmore
C-47 Skytrain

349th Troop Carrier Group
23rd TCS, 312th TCS, 313th TCS, 314th TCS
Barkston Heath
C-46 Commando

53RD TROOP CARRIER WING
Greenham Common

434th Troop Carrier Group
71st TCS, 72nd TCS, 73rd TCS, 74th TCS
Fulbeck, Welford, Aldermaston
C-47 Skytrain

435th Troop Carrier Group
75th TCS, 76th TCS, 77th TCS, 78th TCS
Langar, Welford
C-47 Skytrain

436th Troop Carrier Group
79th TCS, 80th TCS, 81st TCS, 82nd TCS
Bottesford, Membury
C-47 Skytrain

437th Troop Carrier Group
83rd TCS, 84th TCS, 85th TCS, 86th TCS
Balderton, Ramsbury
C-47 Skytrain

438th Troop Carrier Group
87th TCS, 88th TCS, 89th TCS, 90th TCS
Welford, Greenham Common
C-47 Skytrain

---

* The IX Air Defense Command's mission was to provide Anti-Aircraft Artillery, Radar and Barrage Balloons to protect and defend the air bases. The IX Aviation Engineer Command's mission was to gather and use construction equipment to build instant airfields and rehabilitate captured fields for use by the tactical and troop carrier groups.

316th TCG. C-47s with Gliders for Holland.

44th TCSQ/316th TCG. C-47 loading 82nd Airborne for D-Day.

59th TCS/61st TCG C-47 with British paratroopers.

The Ninth Air Force Units on the Continent: Most of the Ninth moved into bases on the Continent as the Allied ground forces pushed the German armies into defeat. The exodus began almost simultaneously when the Allies invaded Normandy on D-Day, 6 June 1944. U.S. Army Air Forces (USAAF) engineers were among the initial assault troops. Their mission was to construct forward operating airfields, known as Advanced Landing Grounds (ALGs), on the continent. As the Allied armies advanced across Europe, several hundred airfields were rebuilt or rehabilitated for use by the Allied air forces.

The responsibility for this task was given to the Ninth Air Force's specially created arm, the IX Aviation Engineering Command. The units within this command were divided into a total of 16 battalions, each composed of sufficient personnel and equipment to construct quickly an airfield or landing ground for a single tactical fighter or bomb group unit.

On D-Day, Normandy, these battalions went ashore alongside U.S. Army infantrymen and headed for pre-selected sites on which to build airfields. Before the end of the day, an emergency landing field was completed at Poupeville, France. By 8 June, a transport field was built at St. Laurent sur Mer (A-21). This was the first American airfield on the European Theater of Operations (ETO).

For security reasons, the airstrips were designated by a coded number rather than by locations. In England, the USAAF installations were identified by three-digit numbers ranging from AAF-1-1 to AAF 925. The continental airfields were also assigned coded numbers. American airfields were assigned A-# (as above A-21), Y-, or R-, number consecutively from 1 to 99. British

Above and below: 833rd Aviation Eng. Battalion. Air Field Construction.

834th and 840th Aviation Engineering Battalions

394th Bomb Group and 861st Aviation Engineering Battalions.

airfields were also consecutively numbered preceded by a B-prefix. Example: B-1, Asnelles sur Mer, France.

By the end of June 1944, eight Ninth Air Force fighter groups were flying tactical bombing missions from ten operational airfields in the Normandy beachhead. By the end of July 1944, all but three of the Ninth Air Force's 20 fighter groups were based on advanced landing grounds on the continent.

By 15 September 1944, the IX Aviation Engineer Command had placed over 80 fields in operation. In late 1944, to lessen the shortage

862nd AES. With equipment.

10th Photo Reconnaissance Group. F-5E Lightning.

401st FS/370th FG. P-38J Lightning.

*Capt. Lindsey
Medal of Honor. B-26*

opportunity was used to clear captured German airfields for use along the armies' routes to allow transport planes to land food, gas, and ammunition, and to continue their evacuation of wounded. By V-E Day, 8 May 1945, 76 of the 126 airfields made operational east of the Rhine River were used strictly for supply and evacuation missions.

In all, the engineers had constructed or rehabilitated over 280 airfields from D-Day to V-E Day.

(Source: 1st Lt. David C. Johnson, *U.S. Army Air Forces Continental Airfield (ETO): D-Day to V-E Day: A Guide to the Airfields Used by the U.S. Army Air Forces During World War II in the European Theater of Operations From 6 June 1944 to 9 May 1945*. Research Division, USAF Historical Research Center, Maxwell Air Force Base, Alabama, 1988.)

of supplies to the Allied ground forces, airfields for C-47 planes became a priority. This allowed the C-47s to deliver ammunition and gasoline, and on the return trips to evacuate wounded to the rear.

By late March, April, and May of 1945, when the German military was waning, every

9th Air Force Today

In 1954, when the 9th was permanently stationed at Shaw AFB, South Carolina, it assumed a role, which it maintains until the present day, of training combat units to meet a broad range of contingencies.

Following the seizure of the U.S. embassy in Tehran in 1979 by Iranians, and the invasion of Afghanistan by Russia, the United States formed a Rapid Deployment Joint Task Force (RDJTF) with the 9th as its air arm. On the last day of December 1982, the RDJTF was inactivated and replaced by the United States Central Command (USCENTAF). The 9th was selected as the US Central Command Air Forces (USCENTAF) and assumed operational control of ongoing air operations in its area of responsibility.

USCENTAF was first tested in 1990 when Iraq invaded Kuwait. During Operation Desert Storm the Air Force played a key role in destroying both Iraq's

356th FSQ/354 FG Medal of Honor.

MEDAL OF HONOR
Lieutenant Colonel James H. Howard, USAAC, January 11, 1944, over Oschersleben, Germany.

CITATION

For conspicuous gallantry and intrepidity above and beyond the call of duty in action with the enemy near Oschersleben, Germany, on January 11, 1944. On that day Colonel Howard was the leader of a group of P-51 aircraft providing support for a heavy bomber formation on a long-range mission deep in enemy territory. As Colonel Howard's group met the bombers in the target area the bomber force was attacked by numerous enemy fighters. Colonel Howard, with his group, at once engaged the enemy and himself destroyed a German Me 110. As a result of this attack Colonel Howard lost contact with his group and at once returned to the level of the bomber formation. He then saw that the bombers were being heavily attacked by enemy airplanes and that no other friendly fighters were at hand. While Colonel Howard could have waited to attempt to assemble his group before engaging the enemy, he chose instead to attack singlehanded a formation of more than 30 German airplanes. With utter disregard for his own safety he immediately pressed home determined attacks for some 30 minutes, during which time he destroyed three enemy airplanes and probably destroyed and damaged others. Toward the end of this engagement three of his guns went out of action and his fuel supply was becoming dangerously low. Despite these handicaps and the almost insuperable odds against him, Colonel Howard continued his aggressive action in an attempt to protect the bombers from the numerous fighters. His skill, courage, and intrepidity on this occasion set an example of heroism which will be an inspiration to the Armed Forces of the United States.

air force and decimating its army with minimal loss of life. USCENTAF flew over 29,000 sorties, dropped close to 61,000 tons of ordnance and destroyed 215 enemy aircraft.

In late 1994, when Iraq again began massing troops, USCENTAF responded with Operation Vigilant Warrior. When that crisis ended two months later, many of the aircraft and deployed troops remained to continue their watch.

From 1994 to 2000, in the Middle East, 9th Air Force/USCENTAF continued its support of such operations as Desert Strike, Desert Thunder, and Desert Fox, and it flew humanitarian missions in Somalia, Bosnia, and Haiti.

Upon assuming command of the 9th in January 2000, Lieutenant General Charles F. Wald established goals for what he saw as four critical areas of importance in the Middle East: These areas were Southern Watch; preparation for a major war in the theater; development of a Combined Air Operations Center (CAOC) in Saudi Arabia; and formation of a model program to promote stability and improved interfacing between the various air forces in the region and the USAF. This was accomplished through participation in joint exercises, and planning assistance in such exercises, symposia, a tactical leadership program, and others such as training in weather, medial and disaster response training.

In November 2001, General Wald was succeeded by Lieutenant General T. Michael Moseley, who continues his predecessor's programs in Operation Enduring Freedom, the United States' answer to the September 11, 2001, terrorists attacks, and in Operation Iraqi Freedom, the war against Iraq's former leader, Saddam Hussein, in 2003.

The 9th Air Force, along with the 8th and 12th Air Forces, is a component of the Air Combat Command, with headquarters located in Langley Air Force base, Virginia. Under its present commander, Lt. General T. Michael Moseley, the 9th's components, their locations, and aircraft are:

- 1st Fighter Wing, Langley, AFB, VA, flying F-15C/D aircraft
- 4th Fighter Wing, Seymour Johnson AFB, NC, flying F-15E aircraft
- 20th Fighter Wing, Shaw AFB, SC, flying F-16C/CJ/D aircraft
- 33rd Fighter Wing, Elgin AFB, FL, flying F-15c/D aircraft
- 347th Rescue Wing, Moody AFB, GA, flying HC-130, HH-60 aircraft

(Sources: AIR FORCE magazine: Journal of the Air Force Association, *USAF Almanac 2003*. May 2003, and *A Brief History of 9AF and USCENTAF: 1942-2002*, supplied by Kathi Jones, Historian, 9th AF.)

”The Ninth Air Force Association

In the summer of 1990, 14 men from different parts of the country gathered in St. Louis, Missouri, with the sole purpose of forming an association to preserve the history and traditions of the Ninth Air Force — the unit with which they had served in World War II.

The Founders were:
Leonard Bennett (50 FG)
Harold Crocker (406 FG)
Martin Engler (366 FG)
Fred Fehsenfeld (354 FG)
Laurence C. Gaughren (405 FG)
George Johnson (50 FG)
Lloyd L. Johnson (50 FG)
Edward F. MacLean (362 FG)
Charles F. Mann (362 FG)
Fred Munder (363 FG)
John Peterson (366 FG)
Marvin J. Rosvold (368 FG)
George Wagasky Jr. (365 FG)
John B. Yarger (406 FG)

The 14 originals established the goals which still drive the Ninth AFA:

- To preserve and publicize the history of the Ninth Air Force from its inception in World War II to the present time.
- To honor and memorialize the sacrifices of our comrades and their families.
- To promote fellowship among the survivors, families, and descendants of those assigned to the Ninth Air Force at any time.
- To foster the continuing quest for individual liberty and love of our country.

The *Ninth Flyer*, the association's official voice, was first issued in January 1991. It is still being issued quarterly.

The first formal convention was held in September 1991 in Dayton, Ohio. Since then, conventions have been held in Orlando, Florida (1992); Colorado Springs, Colorado (1993); in Europe and New Orleans, Louisiana (1994); Europe (1995); Las Vegas, Nevada (1996); Fort Walton Beach, Florida (1997); San Diego, California (1999); Omaha, Nebraska (2000); Memphis, Tennessee (2001); Branson, Missouri (2002); and Salt Lake City, Utah (2003).

The association is managed by four officers: President, Vice-President, Secretary, and Treasurer, and a Board of Directors of 11 members. The president also serves on the Board.

AIRFIELDS IN EUROPE ON WHICH 9th AIR FORCE FLYING UNITS WERE BASED

FRANCE

B-92	Abbeville/Drucat		Jullouville		St. Cyr
B-54	Achiet	A-68	Juvincourt	A-64	St. Dizier
B-48	Amiens/Glisy		La Bozoge		St. Germain
A-76	Athis	A-69	Laon/Athies	A-29	St. James
A-7	Azeville	A-70	Laon/Couvron	A-36	St. Leonard
	Beauchamps	A-19	La Vielle		St. Mere Eglise
A-61	Beauvais/Tille	A-57	Laval		St. Maurice-aux-
A-60	Beaumont-sur-Oise	A-35	Le Mans		Riches-Hommes
A-6	Beuzeville-au-Plain	A-9	Le Molay	A-43	St. Marceau
A-48	Bretigny		Le Repas	A-1	St. Pierre du Mont
A-16	Brucheville	A-20	Lessay		St. Pois
Y-4	Buc	A-12	Lignerolles		St. Sauveur-Lendelin
	Buhl	A-45	Lonray		Sarreguemines
A-74	Cambrais/Niergnies	Y-6	Lyons/Bron		Somme-Suippes
	Canisy		Maillebois	Y-1	Tantonville
A-10	Carentan	A-15	Maupertus	A-90	Toul/Croix-de-Metz
A-3	Cardonville	A-17	Meautis	A-13	Tour-en-Bessin
	Chapelle	Y-34	Metz/Frescaty	A-46	Toussus-le-Noble
A-40	Chartres	A-55	Melun/Villaroche		Valenciennes
A-39	Chateaudun	A-38	Montreuil		Valognes
A-71	Clastres	A-80	Mourmelon-le-Grand	A-33	Vannes
	Colombieres	Y-42	Nancy/Essey	Y-28	Verdun/Charny
A-59	Cormeilles-en-Vexin		Nehou	A-42	Villacoublay
A-94	Conflans/Doncourt	A-11	Neuilly/Isigny	A-63	Villeneuve/Vertus
A-58	Coulommiers/Voisins	A-66	Orconte		Vittel
	Courcy	A-50	Orleans/Bricy	B-50	Vitry-en-Artois
	Couterne	A-47	Orly	A-67	Vitry-le-Francois
A-81	Creil	A-44	Peray		Vouilly
A-14	Cretteville	A-72	Peronne		
A-2	Cricqueville-en-Bessin	A-65	Perthes		**BELGIUM**
	Dampierre	A-8	Picauville	B-70	Antwerp/Deurne
A-83	Denain/Prouvy		Poilley		Arlon
A-4	Deux Jumeaux	B-44	Poix	Y-29	Asch
Y-9	Dijon/Longvic	A-28	Pontorson		Celles
Y-7	Dole/Tavaux	A-79	Prosnes	A-84	Chievres/Mons
A-41	Dreux/Vermouillet	A-23	Querqueville	A-87	Charleroi
	Epinal	A-62	Reims/Champagne	A-78	Florennes/Juzaine
A-31	Gael	A-27	Rennes/St. Jacques		Gosselies
A-26	Gorges	A-98	Rosieres-en-Haye		Ham
	Gussainville	A-82	Rouvres/Etain	A-89	Le Culot
	Haguenau	A-73	Roye/Amy	A-93	Liege/Bierset
		B-24	St. Andre-de-l'Eure	Y-47	Namur

Y-32	Ophoven	R-9	Erfurt/Bindersleben	R-82	Munich/Reim
A-92	St. Trond	R-11	Eschwege	Y-56	Munchen-Gladbach
	Spa		Euskirchen	Y-94	Munster/Handorf
	Stree		Frankenburg		Nesselwang
	Tongres	Y-74	Frankfurt/Eschborn	Y-62	Neidermennig
	Verviers	Y-73	Frankfurt/Rhein Main		Nordholz
	Vuel	Y-86	Fritzlar	Y-64	Ober Olm
	Zwartburg	R-28	Furth		Oberstein
		R-30	Furth/Industriehaven		Pffafengrund

HOLLAND

		R-77	Gablingen	R-66	Regensburg/Profening
Y-55	Venlo	Y-90	Giebelstadt	R-75	Schleissheim
Y-44	Maastricht/Beek		Gmund	R-79	Schongrau
		Y-99	Gutersloh	R-25	Schweinfurt

LUXEMBURG

			Halle	Y-59	Strassfeld
A-97	Sandweiler		Haltern	R-68	Straubing
			Haunstetten	R-50	Stuttgart/Echterdingen

AUSTRIA

		Y-94	Handorf	Y-51	Vogelsang
R-87	Horsching		Heidelberg		Wickenrode
R-88	Innsbruck		Hersfeld	R-7	Weimar
		R-29	Herzogenaurach	Y-80	Wiesbaden

GERMANY

			Holzkirchen	
Y-46	Aachen	Y-91	Hanau/Langendiebach	
	Ahrweiler		Hornel	*Notes:*
R-45	Ansbach	R-10	Illesheim	A signifies US usage
	Arolsen		Kaiserslauten	B signifies mainly RAF usage
R-84	Augsburg	R-12	Kassel/Rothwesten	Y signifies airfields taken over by US and French troops advancing from southern France
	Bad Godesberg	Y-54	Kelz	
	Bad Wildungen		Kempten	
	Bamberg	R-6	Kitzingen	
R-26	Bayreuth/Bindlach	R-78	Landsberg	
	Berkersheim	R-2	Langensalza	R signifies airfields in Germany occupies by USAAF
	Berlin/Tempelhof	R-59	Leipheim	
R-37	Braunschweig/Waggum	Y-83	Limburg-am-der-Lahn	
R-38	Braunschweig/Broitzen	Y-98	Lippstadt	*Source:* John F. Hamlin, Support and Strike, Petersborough, England, 1991.
R-42	Buchschwabach	Y-79	Mannheim/Sandhofen	
Y-76	Darmstadt		Marburg	
Y-43	Duren			

THE ENGINEER AVIATION REGIMENTS AND BATTALIONS

Brief details of the Engineer Aviation Brigades, Regiments, and Battalions are given below:

Brigades:

1st Engineer Aviation Brigade:
    Activated 1.8.44 as a means of decentralising control; worked in close proximity to TAC and Army which it supported.

2nd Engineer Aviation Brigade:
    as 1st EAB

3rd Engineer Aviation Brigade:
    Activated winter 1944/45

Regiments:

922nd Engineer Aviation Regiment:
    (no details available)

923rd Engineer Aviation Regiment:
    Arrived in France 9.44; employed on airfields on the southern front in support of French 1st Army and US 7th Army.

924th Engineer Aviation Regiment:
    Arrived in UK 7.43; built 28 airstrips in England in 12 months; to France on D+32; built or rebuilt 47 airfields on the Continent; after the Rhine crossing detachments moved with infantry to repair S&E airfields for rapid use.

925th Engineer Aviation Regiment:
    Sometime based at Great Barrington in England; a arrived at Omaha Beach on 2.7.44; built 77 airstrips in ten months; followed the army east via Paris to winter in the Metz area, then pushed into Germany, ending at Munich.

926th Engineer Aviation Regiment:
    Originally based at Honington with the 8th Air Force, for which it carried out 28 jobs; then moved to Great Barrington, with practice moves to Wethersfield and Cokethorpe; landed in France on D+5; followed the Army from Cherbourg to Pilsen in Czechoslovakia; built 76 airfields.

Battalions:

816th Engineer Aviation Battalion:
    Was in the UK for 18 months building 8th Air Force bases; transferred to 9th Air Force; operated in France from D+8; built airstrip A-3, Cardonville; advanced through France into Germany, where it built eight S&E airstrips in three days.

818th Engineer Aviation Battalion:
    Arrived on Utah Beach on 30.6.44; followed the advance through France to Luxemburg and Nancy; built 18 airfields in France and twelve S&E strips east of the Rhine.

819th Engineer Aviation Battalion:
    Built Andrews Field for the 8th Air Force before transferring to the 9th; elements landed in Normandy on D-Day; built ten ALGs and 14 S&E air-strips; rebuilt three enemy airfields.

820th Engineer Aviation Battalion:
    Was employed for two years on airfield construction in England; arrived on Omaha Beach on D+1; followed the advance into Belgium and across the Rhine.

825th Engineer Aviation Battalion:
    (no details available)

826th Engineer Aviation Battalion:
    Arrived in Normandy on D+6; Built A-10, Carentan, in six days while under artillery fire; built airfields behind the US 7th and 9th Armies; had moved deep into Germany by VE-Day.

830th Engineer Aviation Battalion:
    Spent 22 months working for the 8th Air Force before joining the 9th; moved to Normandy and built 13 airfields.

832nd Engineer Aviation Battalion:
    Built Glatton airfield and Abotts Ripton Depot for the 8th Air Force before moving to the 9th's ALGs in Kent, which it then maintained; arrived in France on D+24; built ten airfields and 16 S&E airstrips and maintained nine others.

833rd Engineer Aviation Battalion:
: Worked for the 8th Air Force before transferring to the 9th; arrived at Omaha Beach on 30.6.44; no further information.

834th Engineer Aviation Battalion:
: Constructed Matching airfield for 8th AF; assigned to 9th AF 12.43; carried out training at Chisledon, Torquay, Matching and Great Barrington; landed Omaha Beach on D-Day; built ELS at St. Laurent-sur-Mer (first C-47 landed early 9.6.44); constructed St. Pierre du Mont, Le Molay, Courtils, Lombron; refurbished St. Trond (Belgium) and various airfields in France; Built Niedermendig, Ailertchen and Limburg in Germany and Pilsen in Czechoslovakia and rebuilt Erfurt.

837th Engineer Aviation Battalion:
: Saw service in Africa, Italy and the MTO before joining IX EC in 3.45; worked at Marseilles.

840th Engineer Aviation Battalion:
: Arrived in Normandy early 7.44; advanced with the Army through France to Stuttgart.

843rd Engineer Aviation Battalion:
: Arrived in Normandy on D+25; Built 40 air fields; was in Munich on VE-Day.

846th Engineer Aviation Battalion:
: Arrived in Normandy on 16.7.44; completed airstrip A-13 (Tour-en-Bessin) in ten days; then moved through France to end at Bremen.

847th Engineer Aviation Battalion:
: Was with 1st TAF until 2.45; built medium-bomber airfields at Lyon and Dijon.

850th Engineer Aviation Battalion:
: Arrived on Utah Beach on D+14; advanced through France and into Germany.

851st Engineer Aviation Battalion:
: Maintained seven ALGs in SE England before moving to France and on into Germany.

852nd Engineer Aviation Battalion:
: Arrived in UK 5.43; moved to Normandy on D+37; then advanced through France and into Germany.

859th Engineer Aviation Battalion:
: Built an 8th Air Force airfield before moving to France; finally into Germany.

861st Engineer Aviation Battalion:
: Arrived in UK 5.43; built Boreham airfield; then employed on maintenance of 8th Air Force bases.

862nd Engineer Aviation Battalion:
: Was in the UK for 14 months (at Birch from 26.4.44); then moved through France into Belgium; at one time maintained all USAAF airfields in Belgium and Holland.

876th Airborne Engineer Aviation Battalion:
: Was at Sole Common, Berkshire, by 7.43 and became the first unit assigned to IX EC; carried out mainly maintenance on airfields in France, Belgium and Germany.

877th Airborne Engineer Aviation Battalion:
: Arrived in the UK (Bruern Abbey) in 3.44; moved to Normandy on D+30; built A-15, Maupertus, the first B-26 airfield on the Continent; was involved in the construction or maintenance of 66 airfields on the Continent.

878th Airborne Engineer Aviation Battalion:
: Arrived in the UK (Sole Common, Berkshire) in 3.44; apparently did not see any active service until it was involved in Operation Market Garden at Arnhem.

Source: John F. Hamlin, *Support and Strike*, Petersborough, England, 1991.

Courtesy of Loren W. Herway

NINTH AIR FORCE
SPECIAL STORIES

510th FTR SQ 405TH FTR GROUP, 9TH AF-ETO. (Courtesy of Howard J. Curran)

Roer River Dam - November 1944. (Courtesy of James T. Lee)

A Roaring Homecoming
by Robert V. Brulle

As we walked along the war scarred cobble stone streets in Oordegem, Belgium, my anticipation and excitement could hardly be contained as I recognized my old school and church I had attended. "Hey! There's my old school and church," I exclaimed to my companion, Chuck. "Did you know that church is over 100 years old—come on, we go this way." It was a wet and cloudy October day in 1944 as I led Chuck through the well-cultivated fields of the Flanders area of Belgium. Fifteen years after leaving Belgium and immigrating to America with my parents, I was returning to my Belgium home. I was impatient to get a glimpse of the old house and anxious to learn how my relatives had survived the long ordeal of German occupation, all contact with them having been severed since 1939.

I was a U.S. Army fighter pilot and had been flying combat missions from England and France. When Belgium was liberated by the British Army I was stationed at Laon, France, and at the first opportunity hitch-hiked my way to Belgium. On this first trip my flying buddy, Chuck Bennett, accompanied me, and as we walked the 1-1/2 miles from town to my old home, many remembrances came back. "Those minnows are still there," I laughingly said to Chuck as we passed the small brook where I spent hours trying to catch them. "There's the old windmill," I pointed out. "I used to go there with my uncle to get our wheat ground into flour." It was still standing but obviously was not used anymore. (It has now been restored and is an official Belgium landmark.) We passed the big meadow that usually flooded during the winter, making an ice pond where my older brother pushed me around on a battered chair. The soggy ground was now occupied by a contingent of Canadian troops. The pictures I saw of WWI soldiers slogging through the muck during the Passchendaele battle, was not unlike those dutiful soldiers trudging around in that miserable, muddy field.

The old house finally came into view. Not only that, I recognized several relatives standing in front talking. My relatives turned and looked curiously at Chuck and I as we approached, wondering why American officers would come there. They obviously did not recognize me, having changed considerably since they last saw me when I was six years old. As we came closer I addressed them in Flemish, still tinged with the local dialect. "Ik ben Robert Vanden Brulle van Oordegem en bringenju vele complementen van myn famalie in Amerika." (I am Robert Vanden Brulle from Oordegem and bring you many good wishes from my family in America.) Boy! What a commotion that caused! They couldn't believe I was Robert. In their

(Courtesy of Robert V. Brulle)

eyes I was still a little boy, and must be Albert my older brother. With many gestures accompanying my halting Flemish, I finally convinced them who I was. Shortly, the whole community there asking questions and wanting to meet me.

Everyone of my relatives had survived the war. One had been bombed out of his home. Another, as a Belgium soldier, had been captured by the Germans early in the war, but after a six month imprisonment had escaped and had not been bothered by the Germans as he helped my aunt and uncle tend their small farm. My relatives looked fairly healthy, and upon questioning stated that they fared pretty well during the war since they were able to grow much of their own food. Their clothes were threadbare and shabby, but clean. My aunt and uncle, that I had lived with before coming to America, still dressed as the couple in the Jean Francois Millet painting, "The Angelus."

My questions were smothered by my relatives' eagerness to find out about my family and me. They also wondered how I could be an officer, when even the burgomaster's son was only a sergeant in the Belgium army. (At that time the class differences were still very prevalent and your rank in the army was proportional to your status position in the community. My relatives, as common farmers, could only expect to be privates.) My buddy, Chuck, was also surrounded by my questioning relatives, but could only shake his head and keep repeating the words, "niet verstaan." The only controversy of the reunion occurred when I mentioned I was a fighter pilot. They were absolutely stunned and could not believe that I would have chosen to do such a dangerous job.

Also of interest were the musette bags of cigarettes, candy bars, and other goodies Chuck and I brought them. They liked everything we brought, but none of the grownups liked chewing gum. It was a sad parting that evening, but I promised to come again and also buzz them in my P-47 Thunderbolt Fighter.

A week later, flying a combat certification check of a repaired P-47, I proceeded to Oordegem and gave them a buzz job. I flew low, rolled, stunted and wagged my wings to my relatives standing outside. I also looked over the entire area. Several weeks later, I learned about the chaos I had caused by that buzz job. The people in the area thought I was a German aircraft looking for a worthwhile strafing target. The local commuter train stopped and the people leaped into the ditches. Several factories in the adjacent town of Wettern shut down as the workers scrambled to the air raid shelter. The Sisters (Catholic nuns) also let the children out of school, however, their motive was to let the children watch the "flying fool."

News of my visit had been circulated in school by my young cousins, and all the students had been anxiously anticipating the air show.

That first buzz job helped spread the news about the local boy who was a fighter pilot. On an overnight visit I accompanied my cousin to all the taverns in the area. I vaguely remember both of us weaving home on bicycles with two flat tires, singing away as we rode along the pitch dark cobble stone roads. (24 years later I accompanied the same cousin to the same taverns and got reacquainted with many of the same people—only used a car for that sojourn. Many people still related, with glee, the chaos and concern I had caused during that first buzz job.)

I visited and buzzed my home town several more times during the next few months. Every time that I buzzed my old home I stayed above two large trees by the side of the house. I estimated they were 45 feet apart, and since the wing span of a P-47 is 39 feet, I should be able to fly between them. Before leaving Europe for home, I was determined to give them one last buzz job that they would never forget. From 12,000 feet I did a split-S (half roll with a diving pull-out) and applied war emergency power to the engine generating 2,600 horsepower. At a speed over 500 mph, I flew two feet-over the house between the trees. As I pulled up I saw my relatives storming out of the house. I then came around wagging my wings good-by. They were all outside waving at me. Anyway, at that time, I thought they were just waving at me.

Six weeks later when I got home to Chicago, a letter from my aunt in Belgium was already there. It read in part, "Please write and tell Robert not to fly over us so fast and low again." (My relatives could not write directly to me in the American Army since I had no local European address.) My aunt then related what happened on my farewell buzz job: "The ceiling fell down, the cow stopped giving milk, the chickens stopped laying eggs, and worst of all the dog, that pulled their milk wagon, ran away." I caused a minor calamity. Even when I visit them now, some of the younger folks still remember it. They admit, however, they will never forget it. It was a roaring climax, a little overdone perhaps, to a joyous homecoming.

Bombing Missions Experiences
by John P. Crow

I joined the 48th Fighter Group 492nd Sq. at A-92, St. Tround, Belgium in November 1944. We were quartered in what was referred to as the West Point of Belgium.

The first missions I flew were to Aachen, Julich and Duren. We used everything we had to destroy the famous Sports Palace at Julich. There was a flack tower in a huge chimney that we bombed and strafed for a week. After the war I flew back over the area and the damn thing was still there. The main bridge across the Ruhr into Duren was another target that we tried to take out. I drove through Duren after we had pushed the Germans across the Rhine. The entire town was completely destroyed but that damn bridge was still there. I drove across it.

On a mission to Euskirkenn we were to cut the rail lines. On the bomb run at about 5,000 feet I released my bombs just as an 88mm flack exploded right off my wing. The plane almost rolled over on the dive run. I struggled it back and attempted to climb back up, but the right wing kept trying to drop. I kept left stick to stay level and called my flight leader that I was hit and heading home. The plane just would not respond. I called the base for a straight in approach that I was hit and had to land. Permission was granted and as I cleared the trees at the end of the runway the tower screamed that I had a hung bomb on my right wing. It was hanging by the rear hangar nose down and armed. The tower said don't land... I replied that I was hit and couldn't pull up - somehow I got on the ground with the bomb still in place and stopped at the end of the runway and abandoned the jug quickly. There wasn't a soul in sight.

On Sunday Dec. 17, 1944 by my logbook we had a mission to St. Vith logged as an armed recon. We found the roads were full of tanks and trucks heading toward Belgium. The entire squadron had a field day bombing and strafing. On the way back to base one lone ME-109 was spotted. This was the first enemy aircraft many of us had ever seem. The entire squad took after the 109. He led us over some German gun emplacements at very low altitude where we lost our flight leader. Needless to say we reversed directions, hit the very low deck and came home with only one plane lost but several shot up. The weather closed in the next day with the Battle of the Bulge well under way. According to my log we went back to the same area on Sunday, Dec. 24, 1944, and found lines of trucks and tanks stalled on the roads out of fuel. Of course we did not know this. All our flights went down and strafed for miles but could not get many explosions from vehicles without fuel. I just kept following and shooting for several more miles. When I climbed back

492nd Sq. Illishiem, Germany,

up to join the squadron it was nowhere to be seem. I headed back west and noted three P-47s a few miles off my right wing. I turned to join up, and suddenly two FW-190s making an attack on the 47s just loomed in my gun sights. I tied onto one of them with all 50s firing. Apparently I got some hits because he rolled over and headed for the deck with me right on his tail. I followed with two rolls heading to the deck and I lost sight when I came out of the second roll. Being approximately 1,000 feet I decided to get on the deck and head home.

48th Fighter Group.

As I leveled out at about 300 feet I kept getting fire flashes on my wings and thought that my guns were to hot and were firing. I looked over my right shoulder and saw the big round radial nose of a FW-190, ducking I looked over my left shoulder and his buddy was sitting on my left wing. I dropped down to about 100 feet where they would have trouble hitting me. Flashes kept hitting my wings. I dropped down below power lines and just above fences to make it harder to fly and fire. Up ahead was a slight hill with some pine or cedar trees that I knew I had to clear. I waited till the last second to pull up and almost waited too long as I cleared a path of tree tops. The impact scared me and I pulled up a little higher. A 20mm exploded on my instrument panel. At that instant I remembered a speech by Colonel Johnson that when you decide its time to jump don't think about it, get out. I pulled back on the stick, jettisoned the canopy, pushed the throttle full forward with water injection, and began to climb out of the cockpit. While standing in the seat my British radio cord would not release. I jerked with both hands dodged the tail section and jumped. I can remember seeing cracked putty in a window of a building as I left the jug. I have no recollection of riding a parachute down. Apparently the chute broke my fall from head down and I rotated to my feet and hit the ground. I had the rip chord handle in my left hand. I could hear small arms fire from a distance. I left the chute and began running toward the west. After about 1/2 mile I crawled under a hedge row to rest. A civilian with a pistol shot over my head got my attention. I looked around and found a group of civilians encircling my position armed with shotguns and pitch forks.

I dropped my 45 and crawled out of the hedge row and surrendered. One of the civilians noticed the U.S. on my first aid packet on my pistol belt. He asked "you American?"

I replied American pilot. "we Belgians" was like money from home. They took me to a nearby house where a lady washed my face of oil and blood from face lacerations caused by the 20mm shell in the cockpit with me. In a few minutes an infantry captain and troops picked me up. They had been searching the wreckage of my plane for a body. They saw the jug go down but did not see me get out. I was sent to an aid station, patched up, loaded on a jeep and sent back to St. Tround base.

I got back around midnight and found my roommates, Frank Cuff, Doug Hardin, and Bob Hutto drinking my last bottle of Calvert Black Label whiskey that we were saving for Christmas. Needless to say that was my best Christmas.

Our base at St. Tround was in the direct flight line of the German buzz bombs that were directed to Antwerpt, Belgian. During the winter of 1944 almost every night we would hear the putt putt of these bombs going overhead. We had a ringside seat to watch the antiaircraft guns trying to knock them down before they got to Antwerpt. The sky for miles around would light up when the bombs were hit. British typhoons were stationed at this base to shoot down the buzz bombs. Our P-47s were not fast enough to catch them.

In the spring advance to the Rhine River we moved to Y54, Keltz, Germany a wheat field with steel matts for a runway south east of Cologne in late March. From this base we covered the Remeagen bridge crossing. We were about 20 minutes flying time to give ground support to the bridgehead across the Rhine. An unconfirmed story was that the Germans had some operational P-47s and tried to bomb the Remeagen bridge. We had orders not to fly directly over the bridge at any time. The GI's guarding that bridge had orders to shoot first then confirm. We lost Lt. Dundon with a direct 88mm hit while dive bombing ahead of ground troops at the bridgehead.

After the Rhine Pocket was pretty well surrounded we had a mission knock out the German headquarters at Dusseldorf. We had eight P-47s loaded with demolition bombs and the yellow flight was loaded with delayed action bombs and were to skip bomb if red and blue flight failed to destroy target. I was yellow 4 or the last one. We circled the area with broken clouds for several minutes searching for the targeted building. Flight leader Lt. Kresge spotted the building but it had a white cross painted on the roof. He called our controller, "Marmite" requesting orders. After a few minutes "Marmite" ordered "blow it to hell." Red flight went in and dropped bombs everywhere except on target. Flack was getting pretty hot. Blue flight went down with same results. Yellow leader and his wingman Lt. Hovde decided to try the skip bombs. Glory be, Lt. Hovde skidded one in the front door and the building utterly collapsed. Yellow 3 and 4 were instructed to jettison bombs and lets go home. I will always be grateful to Lt. Hovde because the flack was really getting hot when he went down.

We flew several missions from late March until mid-April along the Rhine River and consolidating the Rhine Pocket.

On or about 17 April 1944 we moved to R-12, Kassel, Germany. This was a former German air base located on a hill overlooking the city of Kassel. On a mission from Kassel my roommate, the late Frank B. Cuff, was shot down near the advancing infantry. He was picked and flown back to base in an artillery observation cub loaded with a case of German snoops "German whiskey" that the infantry gave him in appreciation for what the jugs were doing. Needless to say he was pretty well "loaded" too. We all had "glad you made it." After a couple of weeks we moved to R10, Illesheim, Germany, for the final days of the war.

We flew several missions to buzz the POW camps that were down in the alps. The war ended as we got the new P-47Ns with the compressibility flaps.

After quite a bit of conversation as to whether these flaps would work a major and I decided to test them out. We climbed to about 35,000 feet and split S down at full throttle. The air speed indicator was red lined at 500 mph; it hit the peg at 550 with complete condensation blocking any visibility; the altimeter was spinning down; I had all my strength trying to pull back the stick; the plane was shaking like a rub-board; at 20,000 1 pulled back on the throttle; flipped the compressibility flaps and passed out; I came to at approximately 18,000 feet on my back; I slowly rolled over and very casually came back to base. The flaps worked! I have a great respect for Chuck Yeager.

Luck of the Irish
By Howard J. Curran

In September 1944, I was an "evadee" in the area of Pont-A-Mousson, which is midway between Metz and Nancy on the Moselle River in eastern France. I had been shot down on September 12th while flying my 95th mission. It also was the first mission for the 510th Squadron from our new base at St. Dizier.

Sept. 1944, Capt. Howard Curran (Evadee) and French Benefactor behind enemy lines at Pont A Massoun, France. (Courtesy of Howard J. Curran)

During the afternoon on a sunny French day, I was in the company of my French benefactor, "Francois Lertex," a young Frenchman who had been active in the French Resistance and was still risking his life by helping me evade capture by the Germans.

For the past few days, the Germans to the east and the Americans to the west had been having an artillery duel, and we had become so accustomed to it that we would identify the shells passing overhead by the sound.

We were enjoying the lovely September afternoon in the stone-walled courtyard behind the house where I was being hidden when a "short round" from the Americans fell in the courtyard near us. Luckily, it fell just beyond us, and the concussion and shrapnel from the exploding shell fragmented into the stone wall. Later we determined that it exploded less than 20 feet from us.

The moral of this experience is that except for "the luck of the Irish," my flying career would have ended in a French courtyard by friendly artillery.

WWII Experiences
by Arthur C. Derocher

After serving 2-1/2 years in the CCC I joined the regular Army on September 23, 1940, right after my 21st birthday. My hometown was Avon, MA.

In September 1941 I was an MP at Westover Field, Chicopee, MA. I left with a group for Gander Air Base for the North Atlantic Patrol. We had B-17s. We were on one side of the runway, with the West Canadian Hospital and Royal Canadian Air Force. Also on the base were the Prince Edward Island Highlanders Infantry and the Royal Canadian Ferry group which flew planes to England.

While I was at Gander Molotov stopped by in a big Russian bomber. He was going to Washington to meet with President Roosevelt.

Our planes going to England stopped at Gander. Also USO troupes, Joan Blondell was a member of one of these troupes and I was among those in a group picture taken with her a month before December 7, 1941.

The kitchen was looking for cooks, so I signed up to learn to cook.

The Senior News was looking for stories. "Where were you on December 7, 1941?" I sent in a story of where I was and they printed it. On that day I was in the PX when over the radio it was announced that Japan had bombed Pearl Harbor. In my story I forgot to mention that I had had my picture taken with Joan Blondell.

On December 20, 1942 we were sent back to the States. We ended up at Grenier Field, New Hampshire, in January 1943. There were about four of us from Gander Air Base who signed up to go to Westover Field. We were assigned to the 362nd Fighter Group. Already there were the 376th and 377th, and we were assigned to the 378th Fighter Squadron. After training we ended up at Camp Shanks, NY. On November 12, 1943 we boarded a train for the ferry. We went out on the water on a misty, lousy night. When we arrived at the New York port the Red Cross was there, and then we boarded the *Queen Elizabeth* on November 23, 1943. We landed on November 30, 1943 and went to AAF Station 159, Wormingham Cochester, Essex, England.

Our group flew for the 8th Air Force. Then we went to AAF Station 412. This was Headcorn, Mardstone, Kent England, April 16, 1944.

Courtesy of Russell Fairbanks.

Our group was making a name for itself, known as Mogin's Maulers. D-Day, June 6, 1944, our fighters were on the runways waiting to be called. Our fighters carried bombs, 50-caliber guns. If going on long missions they carried a belly tank of fuel. On D-Day I had a school pal who was on the 3rd Wave. He lost his guitar. Our group split up in two echelons. They went ahead and set up the A Strip, and the B Echelon went next to join up. We left Southhampton on an Indian ship and landed at Omaha.

Our first air strip was Balleroia A-12. We slept in foxholes on cots. They were big and we were strafed by Midnight Charlie (Germany). We went for a hike one day and came upon an English outfit. They were on one side and on the other side were the Germans - watching one another. Also at Balleroia there was a reporter, Austen Lake. He interviewed me "A soldier from Rhode Island." We were in the Ninth Task Force.

I was made a sergeant before I left for overseas.

From Balleroia we went to A-27 Rennes (St. Jacques). Then September 1944 to Rhiems (Prosness). While there I saw the Rhiems Cathedral, very large. November 8, 1944 we went to Etain (Roevres). This was Patton's Headquarters. One day we went to a field hospital, knee-deep in mud. In December 1944 I was transferred to a Replacement Depot at LeBourget Air Port. While there I did guard duty on the air strip.

In January 1945 I had enough points to go back to the States. At Atlantic City, NJ the Air Force was in the best hotels and after getting physicals we were shipped out to Kearny Air Force Replacement Depot. You could sign up for a train ride taking men to California or Vancouver, WA. I took that one. Had to watch while cooking. Had to watch the kettles going up the mountains. It was fun.

When I got back I signed up to get out. I had to go back to Atlantic City. I was honorably discharged September 20, 1945. Now I belong to the Air Force Sergeants Association.

Oh, God... Don't Let It Cartwheel
by William B. Foster

The girl was young and pretty, but Lt. Bill Foster had other things on his mind.

"Who am I being held by?" he asked her, as hard-eyed, armed men directed him to a seat. The girl's eyes were sympathetic, but she knew little English. The soldiers, she said, were Germans. The day, which had started badly, was ending even worse. Another day in a long war. December 23, 1944. He was 22 years old.

The young fighter pilot could not know that 54 years later and 10,000 miles away, this awful day would come back to him in a very warm and unexpected way.

Today, in his late 70s, Foster lives quietly in Hutchinson, Kansas with his wife Beulah. He remembers those long-ago events, and the girl, with crystal clarity.

"When I opened the throttle and headed down the runway that morning, I just had a feeling that this was it," he recalls.

Pilots, especially combat pilots, are not given to vague fears and alarms, but once in a while fate seems to whisper in your ear. And so it seemed on this morning.

Operating from A-82, a forward airstrip near Etain, France, Foster was flying a Republic P-47D Thunderbolt. The big fighter bore the blue-painted nose of the 378th Fighter Squadron, an Army Air Corps serial number and squadron letters G8-Q. That was the official designation. Unofficially, she was dubbed "Street Cleaner," in recognition of her many strafing missions. She was now a war-weary squadron spare, flown by whoever needed her. With his own battle-damaged ship down for repairs, Foster had drawn her for today's mission. His 13th mission.

Climbing away from the runway, he tried to shake off the concerned feeling, putting it down to "13th Mission" jitters. Bad weather had kept the fighters grounded for a week, but this morning's mission was simple enough: escort C-47 cargo planes as they dropped badly needed supplies to General McAuliffe's besieged troops at Bastogne, then strafe and bomb "targets of opportunity." Foster, a replacement pilot who had only 12 previous missions with the 378th, had seen plenty of action in his dozen cracks at the enemy and had acquitted himself well. His bombing and strafing runs had accounted for many trucks, tanks, and other motorized vehicles and a lot of railroad rolling stock, including a double-header. He had seen friends die. And he had nearly died himself. On his 12th mission, he was making a low-level strafing pass when ground fire blew off his right aileron. The right and left ailerons control the aircraft's rolling motion. Instantly, the seven-ton fighter was on its back, Foster fighting instinctively and desperately for control. The ground was very close and rushing by at more than 300 miles per hour. Anything but precisely the right control movements would have been instantly fatal. Later, after the mission, he was unable to explain to his squadron mates or to himself how he was able to right the crippled fighter. He merely shrugs, "Instinct and training, I guess."

But on this day, this 13th mission, he would fly just beyond the limit of his luck. Two hours into the mission, the prophecy that had nagged him at take-off came to frightening fulfillment. "Street Cleaner" was a pile of scrap metal in a farm field in Luxembourg and he was in the hands of the Germans.

After escorting the C-47s to Bastogne then back toward the coast, the fighters had returned to the Bastogne area to attack German positions. Foster, call sign "Firebrick Red 4," was one of a flight of four fighters directed to a place called Hill 507. Several German tanks in fortified position were directing effective fire at American positions. Locating the targets, the P-47s rolled in to attack. Suddenly, things went very wrong

"They were throwing a lot of 20mm stuff at us. Ground fire hit the prop and damaged it pretty bad," Foster recalls. The huge four-bladed propeller was now badly out of balance, setting up severe and dangerous vibration throughout the airplane. Structural failure was a very real possibility.

"The instrument panel was jumping up and down and I was losing altitude. I kept throttling back as much as I could and still keep flying," Foster recalls.

Lt. Dick Law, leading the fighters, knew Foster was in trouble. He called for a heading to get him back across American lines as soon as possible.

"At first I told him I thought I could make it back, but pretty soon I knew I couldn't make it," Foster said. "I had to get her down, fast."

Law radioed their present position in as he watched his friend lose altitude. Foster was now down to about 300 feet and the situation was deteriorating rapidly. Time and luck had run out simultaneously. He had to put the airplane on the ground. Now.

Lt. Cliff Saari, on whose right wing Foster had been flying, stayed with him as he went down, flying cover. "I told him I was going to try to belly in. The only spot was a little open patch of ground, maybe about five acres or so, near what looked like a big farmhouse.

Lining the airplane up as well as possible, Foster prepared to belly land the crippled ship. A gear down landing was not possible due to the rough ground. "I opened the canopy so it wouldn't jam and I shut off all the switches and the fuel. I didn't want a fire if I could help it."

Foster, who claims not to have been "overly-religious," remembers the impact and a spontaneous, shouted prayer. "Oh God! Don't let it cartwheel!"

If the airplane caught a wing and cartwheeled, his chances of survival would diminish rapidly. The shouted plea was apparently heard. The P-47 slithered across the snow-covered ground, upright, shedding pieces as it went. A tree sheared the right wing off and the ship slowed sharply. Another tree sliced through the fuselage behind the cockpit, taking off the tail assembly. The huge radial engine separated from its mounts and rolled under the airplane. Foster was thrown violently around the cockpit, and the pummeling left him with neck pain that bothers him yet today. The control stick was wrenched from his grip and flailed side-to-side, beating and bruising the insides of his knees and thighs.

As with many accidents, things seemed to occur in slow motion and with amazing detail. As the airplane slid along toward a narrow road and more trees beyond, Foster recalls seeing something almost comical.

"Some German on a motorcycle was trying to head me off, I guess, and passed less than 50 feet in front of me!"

But, the suicidal soldier was quickly forgotten as Foster's ship disintegrated around him and finally slid to a stop. As dirt and snow settled into the air, he unstrapped himself and got quickly away from the wreckage. Lt. Saari made a low pass to check on him. "I waved to him that I was OK, and ducked into some bushes."

It proved to be a fragile sanctuary. With four to five inches of snow on the ground, the Germans had little difficulty tracking Foster. Within minutes, about half a dozen bayonets poked through the brush.

"I decided pretty quickly that my .45 wasn't going to do me much good, so I took it out and handed it through to them, very gentle," he said.

For Foster, the shooting war was over. Shaken and uncertain, the young officer was just glad to be alive. How quickly the day had changed.

Foster, a pilot, got his first look at the enemy close up. The motley uniforms were unusual enough that he wasn't entirely sure they were German.

He was taken to the nearby farmhouse which, in fact, proved to be a crossroads cafe catering to locals and travelers. The Germans had seized it for a command post and were holding the owners.

The family included a 17-year-old girl, who helped fix meals for the Germans. She was present when Foster was brought in.

"She was wearing a long, loose dress, sort of like a peasant dress, I guess, and I remember it was a bluish-gray color. Her hair was dark and she was nice looking. I remember asking her who I was being held by, but we didn't get to talk very long. I remember she was young, and she looked frightened," he said.

It soon became apparent from the girl's comments that his keepers were members of the Wehrmacht, the German Army. They were quickly asking some nearby officers what to do with their American pilot. Orders were to hold him until nightfall, then move him to the rear.

The girl was sent away. He felt encouraged by her kindness, and proud of her apparent determination. He was also sorry for the fear in her eyes.

As the Germans went about their business, Foster had time to reflect. How could all of this have happened in such a compressed span of time? He had entered the service in November 1942. There followed fast-paced months of primary, basic and advanced flight training. A commission, a set of wings on his chest and the shiny gold bars of a "Shavetail" 2nd Lieutenant symbolized his passage into the fraternity of warriors. Then, a long boat ride to England and assignment to a forward fighter base in France had brought him into harm's way.

Now this. God, he was tired!

Once, Foster asked to step outside to relieve himself. "They took my boots," he said. The Germans knew that without his boots he could not hope to run far in the snow, but with his feet now wet, small patches of skin soon froze. After nightfall, he was marched away by a squad of Germans, headed God knows where.

He would later learn that his impromptu landing field was a place called "Schumann's Eck," or Schumann's Corner. The building was the Cafe Schumann. He thought never to see the place again. But a short way down the road from Schumann's Eck, Foster learned all about irony.

"We were walking along this road and I remember thinking how pretty it was with the snow and the moonlight and all. I was kind of surprised I could find beauty in such a bad situation when suddenly we started taking artillery fire from our guys. Everybody hit the ditches to wait until it was over. Some of it was hitting pretty close. I felt this pain in my butt and figured a piece of rock had hit me. Felt like I was hit with a ball-peen hammer. Then, after a minute, there was no pain at all just a total numbness. When we got up, my foot felt warm. My boot was full of blood." He had survived a terrible crash landing, only to be wounded by comrades miles away.

The shaken Germans gathered their wits and their wounded prisoner and returned to Schumann's Eck, where medics applied Sulfa drugs and a field dressing to his wound. Only after his return to American hands would he learn that a piece of shrapnel had entered his right buttock and stopped just short of his spine.

"The Germans treated me pretty well, really," he recalls. "They had put straw down all over the floor for matting and they made me a bed right there with theirs. The straw was really close to the heating stove. I don't know how they kept from burning the place down."

Foster did not see the girl, and wondered where she was. Someplace safe, he hoped. She did not reappear, and he never saw her again.

In the morning, he was marched away again, now limping painfully. Later in the day and miles away at the city of Wiltz, he was deposited at a castle-like building serving as a German field hospital.

And for Foster, irony seemed to follow irony. Lying in the hospital with other prisoners the following day, he happened to glance out the window at just the right moment. The bittersweet scene is still etched in his mind.

"The hospital looked out over a little valley. As I looked out the window, I saw Dick Law's airplane make a pass right up that valley. Right in front of me!"

Merry Christmas.

Several days later he was marched away again.

Shortly thereafter, back home in Abbyville, Kansas, his mother got the terrible telegram every mother dreads. "The War Department regrets to inform you…" But, in this case, it indicated only that he was missing in action and promised further details when available.

Much lay ahead for Foster. Days of marching, pain, solitary confinement, interrogation (on his birthday, January 7), and even a bit more irony. The Germans had taken Foster's flying suit, explaining that it was for his protection. German civilians had several times attacked and killed downed allied fliers. He appreciated his captors' foresight when he saw a large billboard with the word "Achtung! Jabo!" (Attention! Devil!) in bold print, warning Germans to beware of a particular danger. The message was written beneath a large picture of a P-47.

Eventually, after many miles, the marching came to an end and there followed a five-day train ride in drafty boxcars through war-ravaged Germany. During the trip, Foster was given yet another opportunity to wonder at his own survival.

"On January 14th, we were sitting on a siding at the Berlin railroad marshalling yards when the air-raid sirens went off. They got us out of there just ahead of the bombs. Later, we learned we were the last train out of the yards before the bombers leveled the place," he said.

Finally – Stalag Luft I - a prison camp for allied fliers at Barth, Germany. The camp, north of Berlin near the Baltic Sea, was isolated, bleak and in the grip of winter. He was placed in a large barracks room with 23 other officers. Three were P-47 pilots. One was a P-38 pilot. The others were bomber crews - pilots, co-pilots, navigators and bombardiers from B-17s, B-24s and B-26s. Some were sick and all were malnourished.

Seventy kilometers (43 miles) to the east at a place called Peenemunde, Dr. Wehrner Von Braun was building V-2 rockets in an underground factory.

The Germans allowed Foster, through the Red Cross, to get a short note to his mother. On February 27, she received a telegram from the War Department stating that short-wave radio operators had picked up a message read on a German propaganda broadcast. "From Lt. William Foster: Dear Mom—I am alright—there is nothing to worry about—stay in touch with the Red Cross—Love, Bill."

Months of boredom, cold, bad food and dysentery followed. Thoughts of family and home were constant. Bonds of friendship were forged between men who had suffered much. And through it all, the memory of a girl, seen briefly, under the worst of circumstances. A girl whose eyes had spoken out wordless encouragement and friendship. A girl whose own situation evoked reciprocal concern on Foster's part. How had fate dealt with her? How had the Germans dealt with her?

Finally, Freedom. On the 30th day of April 1945, advancing Russian troops overran the Germans, who fled the prison camp. Foster and his companions were transferred to American hands. A few days later, operating from a nearby abandoned German airfield, B-17 bombers flew the former POWs to France.

By June, Foster was back home in Kansas. Hailed on his return, he reacted as many returnees did, sharing some things, keeping others inside. But a tiny corner of his memory was quietly dedicated to a girl in Luxembourg.

As normalcy returned to his world, he found himself a civilian, wondering what to do with the rest of his life. A flying job presented itself, so he got his commercial pilot's license. "The Humble Oil Company down in Texas was hiring guys to fly oil drilling equipment into Central and South America," he said.

"After I got down there and got a look at those beat up old C-47s they wanted us to fly, I wanted no part of that." He had walked away from one crashed airplane. Tempting fate further seemed imprudent.

He returned to Abbyville, and the family occupation - wheat farming. In April 1947, he married Beulah Dunn. He had been her first date in Junior High School. Three daughters followed: Cassandra, Sally and Janet. Harvest followed harvest for the next 48 years until ill health, which had slowed him for some time, forced his retirement in 1995.

Through the years, Foster stayed in touch with his wartime comrades. Grey now, and thinned in ranks, they hold annual reunions and remind each other what stout fellows they were. For a while, they are young again. And after the backslapping, the drinks and the hell-for-leather stories, there often comes, in the mellow hours of the evening, certain faraway looks.

"You know, there was this girl in Luxembourg... There was nothing romantic in it. Nothing sexy. Just a memory. How many times over the years had her face come before him? He hoped she had survived the war.

Then, in May 1998, a phone call. "A friend, Chuck Mann, one of the guys in our fighter group, lived in Memphis, Tennessee," Foster said. "He called me and said he had gotten an e-mail from a guy named John Derneden in Luxembourg and the guy was asking about me."

Derneden, an officer in the Luxembourg military, is also a military historian researching World War II crash sites in his tiny country. Through a copy of the 362nd Fighter Group's unit history book, *Mogin's Maulers,* he had been able to link Foster's name and squadron, the 378th to G8-Q and the crash site. "I wrote to him, and he was thrilled to death," Foster said.

Derneden had a few thrills for Foster, too. The girl at the cafe had indeed survived the war. Derneden knows her well. Her name is Anna Theis. Now 71, she still lives near Schumann's Eck. And she remembers Foster.

In a subsequent letter, Derneden wrote, "She told me that she can remember very well that young, tall, good-looking American pilot. She also remembered that you asked her where you had landed and who were the troops that captured you." Foster, who is five foot seven inches tall, claims not to have felt very tall, nor particularly good-looking on that day.

Amazingly, she had also taken pictures of the wreckage of "Street Cleaner" just after the crash. The Germans had temporarily taken her freedom, but not her camera. Derneden had enclosed photocopies of the pictures. There is no doubt as to the identity of the airplane. The identifying letters G8-Q show clearly in the photos. Other photos showed G8-Q after farmers had removed it from the original site. These photos, taken at close range, showed Foster the true measure of his fortune. The cannon fire that had destroyed his propeller had also ripped through the fuselage inches behind the cockpit seat.

"I had no idea I'd been hit anywhere but the prop," he said. "Seeing that sent shivers down my back. Kind of gives you a creepy feeling."

He also learned something unknown to him at the time of the crash. The crash site was only three miles from American lines.

Soon Derneden sent Foster a book on the wartime history of Schumann's Eck. The book contains Anna's picture of the crash site, with photo credit to her. Pictured also is a War Memorial, erected near the crash site. There is also a picture of Anna, herself.

The book, however, is in German. Foster does not speak German. Foster turned to local Hutchinson attorney R.J. Kleinherenbrink, who is Dutch, but he is fluent in several languages, including German. He kindly agreed to translate for Foster.

"I'm glad to help. You fought for my country, too," he said. A meeting at Kleinherenbrink's office was arranged. As Kleinherenbrink translated, time seemed to slip away for Foster. Sitting in the comfortable law office, he listened almost dreamily as the attorney read. The matter-of-fact recounting of a long-ago war in a far-away place filled him with surging emotion. Looking back across the years, he saw again the shattered airplane, the face of the enemy and the young girl.

Their brief encounter so long ago seemed frozen in time. How incredible that he had lived in her memory, as she had in his, these 54 years. How happy he was just to know she had survived those awful days.

Returning home, he was already composing his next letter to Luxembourg. Would Derneden be seeing Anna soon? How is her English these days? Could she communicate directly with Bill? How nice it would be if he could only hear from her. How nice, indeed. The first week of January 1999 brought a letter from Anna!

Kleinherenbrink translated: "Dear Mr. Foster: I am the girl who was 17 years old, the girl who talked to you after your accident here with us. I thank Mr. Derneden for your address and sending you his (book). A small token after so many years. Enclosed (is) a picture of when I was 17 (now 71). Enclosed (is) a picture of the crash site, which you probably already have. Enclosed (is) a picture of the house "café" Schumann then and now. Best wishes and greetings from Luxembourg. Anna Theis"

Included with the letter was the original crash photo of G8-Q, with a bit of rubber cement still adhering to the back. It had obviously been carefully removed from a personal photo album. There was a photo of Anna dated 1944. There were pictures of Schumann's Cafe after Foster's departure; gunfire had stitched pockmarks all across the building; it was blackened and burned and one wall was down. There were also current photos of Schumann's Cafe and the field where Foster crash-landed.

With the exception of an excellent restoration of the cafe, all else in that long-ago scene is remarkably unchanged.

"There's where I went in," Foster said. "Even the trees look the same."

Included also was a piece of white cardboard on which was mounted a beautiful pressed and dried flower. Anna had picked it from the crash site a few months earlier. She mailed it on December 23. The 54th anniversary of their meeting. On the card she wrote: "Greeting from Cafe Schumann. A flower from Luxembourg. Happy New Year. Anna Theis."

A warm and wonderful correspondence is now underway between two people, now grown old and serene, who were once young and frightened. They cherish this unlooked-for reunion in the autumn of their days. A meeting would be wonderful. Perhaps, if time is kind...

And finally, another reunion of sorts. Following Anna's letter, a package arrived from Derneden. Enclosed was a small aluminum inspection plate recovered from G8-Q. It came from just forward of the cockpit windshield on the right side of the airplane. "I thought perhaps you might like to have this," Derneden wrote. Foster held the little fragment of his life and wept.

Postscript: In early March 1999, Bill Foster learned from Chuck Mann's widow that yet another reunion may be possible. She had placed a short note about Foster's correspondence with Derneden in the 362nd Fighter Group's quarterly newsletter. Subsequently, she heard from Foster's former Crew Chief, Staff Sergeant Lester Aurilio. Aurilio's job had been to maintain "Street Cleaner." Now 86, he lives, in Ormond Beach, Florida. "I thought he was killed when the airplane went in," he said. "Nobody told me he had survived."

Foster, who had no idea Aurilio was still alive, called him at his home. "We had quite a talk," he said. They spoke of the war and of "Street Cleaner." They spoke of marriage, families and careers.

"I finally told him I was sorry I tore up the airplane he had worked so hard to keep flying. He kind of lost it then, and I guess I did, too. We both cried a little."

This Is What It's All About
by William B. Foster

Here I am standing at "Parade Rest" among thousands of fellow cadets at the close of the day on this vast drill field awaiting the roaring, vibrating sound of the firing of the cannon, the playing of the National Anthem and the close of the day. From where I stood I could see only acres and acres of cadet hats around me; and above their heads at the far end of field I could just see the top of the flag pole with "OLD GLORY" slightly fluttering in the calm, southern breeze of the evening. There was what we were here for; so that wonderful, beautiful flag could continue to wave. Of the thousands of still statues around me many would never complete their training and still more, a great many more would never be able to enjoy the things that we are fighting for. Here I am, just one lone soldier among the millions whom are actually fighting or in training to bring that great day here sooner. There are also millions of others on the home front working both night and day. And yet there are still others that are shirking their duty as far as the overall effort goes. Suddenly, I was brought out of my "dream" by the tremendous boom of the cannon, A sharp "CALL TO

ATTENTION" and absolute silence as the flag slowly floated out of my view behind the acres of cadets. A lump enters my throat and tears trickle down my cheeks as I think what a beautiful flag this is and what a wonderful country I am a part of.

A Bad Day
Submitted by John O.C. McCrillis

May 6th—another bad day for the group. On the early morning mission, Colonel Mills's (Gp C.O.) ship received a direct hit over the enemy lines and was reported to have exploded before hitting the ground. There were varying opinions as to whether chutes had been seen but it did not seem that anyone could have escaped alive. Later however, after Tunis fell, Captain Marcan was found in a former German hospital there. Still later, word was received from the States that Lt. Zerega was home. Capt. Marcan had lost his right arm and broken both legs but beyond the fact that Lt. Zerega was badly burned, we never had more complete information up to the time this was written (February 1944).

The same day, Capt. Bachrach, flying as co-pilot in a ship of the 486th Squadron, landed the plane with no landing gear and the bomb bay doors open, due to hydraulic failure. The pilot had had his leg nearly severed by a shell and died before he could be extricated. Capt. Bachrach was awarded the Distinguished Flying Cross.

Finally as we sweated out the return of the mission, Lt. Touchstone's ship was seen circling in trouble, bomb bay doors open and the bombs hung. He made a wide circle outside the field, set the automatic pilot, and three chutes were seen. Provost Marshal Thomas and some hastily summoned guards raced out on a search and found the wreck just beyond where Major Whittington had crashed on Easter Sunday.

No trace of the crew could be found although there was a rumor at the British camp, which the ship had just missed in its plunge, that two men had been picked up.

Seven unexploded bombs were located in the area over which the ship was scattered but long search through the tall wheat revealed none of the crew.

Guards were posted. Those guards whose names are now in the limbo of forgotten things, will probably be telling their grandchildren about that day 50 years from now. Due to transportation and other difficulties, they had to stay on the job from around 1100 hours to nearly 2000. It was then dark as only the desert can be dark, there were only the two of them patrolling an area nearly a mile square and, for all they knew, they were in for a night of it.

Back at camp, it was learned that the crew was known to be safe, although Lt. Touchstone had wrenched his back and leg and Lt. Pitkin had broken his ankle on their parachute landings.

Lt. Reed, pilot of the ship following Col. Mills, earned the DFC for his ability and efficiency in avoiding a collision and probably saving the lives of his own crew.

The 9th Air Force - Bombers, 1944-45
Submitted by George Parker

The Largest Single Force Of Medium And Fighter Bombers In The World

In September 1943, the 9th Air Force was re-allocated to Great Britain and on October 15 it was formed into a tactical force of fighters and medium and light bombers. General Brereton was still in command. From a small nucleus in September 1943, it grew rapidly into the largest single force of medium

Back row: Lt. Leroy Touchstone, pilot; Lt. Walter Whitehead, co-pilot; Robert Jones, bombadier. Front row: Benjamin Gentry, tail guner; John McCrillis, radio/gunner.

and fighter bombers in the world. From May 1, 1944 to June 6, 1944, it flew more than 35,000 tactical sorties—more than a thousand a day—in preparation for the D-Day of the Normandy invasion. Its targets were enemy airfields, railroad yards, transportation, coastal gun positions, communications and bridges in an area stretching from the Netherlands to the Pyrenees.

The mission of the 9th Air Force as a tactical arm of the USAF in the United Kingdom, was to gain air superiority over Europe by repeated attacks against enemy aircraft in the air and on the ground, and against enemy installations; to prevent the movement of hostile troops and supplies into the theater of operations or within the theater; and to participate in combined operations of the ground and air forces.

The B-26 Marauder was the chief medium bombardment weapon on the Western Front. Fighter planes used included the P-51, P-38 and P-47.

The first operational commitments of the 9th Air Force in the ETO were against the landing fields and installations of the German Air Force within range of the B-26. These attacks were synchronized with assaults of the 8th Air Force on the aircraft industry in the heart of the Reich which were designated to reduce the increased German fighter strength.

Source: "Highlights of the 9th Air Force," Personnel Narratives Division, Office of Information Services, HQ Army Air Forces, 52 Broadway, New York 4, NY (1946)

The First, and Only Major Monument for the B-26 Marauder
(Medium bomber of WWII)

Dedicated at USAF Air Museum, Dayton, Ohio on September 23, 1988 with a fly over by the only flying B-26 from the Confederate Air Force.

Note: A combat pilot with the 599th Sq/397th Bomb Group, 9th Air Force (1944-45) deserves the credit for successful completion of this monument project He is Richard P. Ellinger.

He chaired a committee, but most of the work and providing the spark plug, was he. The policy was discovered that only one major monument per aircraft would usually be permitted at the Air Museum. Although this had been a project financed by the 397th Bomb Group Association, he recommended that all Marauder units be invited to participate. This was accepted and other units were able to engrave a bench, If desired.

The dedication of this monument was the first time since WWII was ended, when all B-26 units were to gather at one place. One 397th member, a couple weeks prior to the final dedication on

B-26 Marauder Monument

September 23, 1988, took action. A meeting was arranged with representatives from several bomb groups for September 22-23, 1988. The B-26 Marauder Historical Society was named and by-laws adopted on September 23, 1988.

Some 500 B-26 veterans and guests were in attendance for the dedication photo on September 23, 1988. The Initial dedication was held September 4, 1987 before the six-foot wingspan, bronze model was installed.

High Flight
by John Gillespie Magee Jr., RCAF

Oh! I have slipped the surly bonds of earth
And danced the skies on laughter-silvered wings
Sunward I've climbed, and joined the tumbling mirth
Of sun-split clouds and done a hundred things
You have not dreamed of wheeled and soared and swung
High in the sunlit silence. Hov'ring there,
I've chased the shouting wind along, and flung
My eager craft through footless halls of air…
Up, Up the long, delirious, burning blue
I've topped the wind-swept heights with easy grace
Where never lark, or even eagle flew
And while with silent lifting mind I've trod
The high untrespassed sanctity of space
Put out my hand and touched the face of God.

Buchenwald Camp Tour, 1945
by Dick Pierce

Soon after V-E Day mopping up operations in Germany included taking POWs back to France and England.

In May 1945 I was sent to an airfield near Weimar. Fortunately, ground time permitted a motor trip with my crew and Mike Frodyma, a friend and college classmate who worked in the U.S. Postal Service in Paris, to the infamous prison camp, Buchenwald, built in 1933. We passed under the great steel arch adorned with a phrase meaning (I believe) "Right or Wrong - Always The Fatherland." The camp where 56,000 had been annihilated, had been hastily cleaned up but many of the tour guides were former prisoners. Our English speaking guide had been a Polish political prisoner apparently weighing less than 100 pounds and still attired in prison garb.

He led us first across the small parade ground where so many had stood nude for so long in the variable weather conditions. Thence to the barracks buildings where the crowded three-tier shelf-bunks were located. The victims crowded existence was obviously worse than deplorable. Next he took us to see the "shower room" and the ovens as well as the burial pits which were covered or empty by this time.

An hour later we were winging our way to our home base, A-48, at Bretigny-sur-Orge (Home Sweet Home), with most of the comforts of home. For obvious reasons a longer visit would not have better satisfied our curiosity or pleased us more. Sadness was too happy a word here to describe our feelings.

Some Of My Memories
by Ralph L. Sallee

I was born in Hollywood, California in 1922. At 19, I worked as a frame builder at Lockheed building Lockheed Lodestars and did some work on P-38s, I did this at night and went to school in the daytime to acquire enough college to enter the US Army Aviation Cadet program.

I received my wings February 8, 1944 with honors for air-to-air gunnery accuracy.

I believe that as Americans we had some advantage over European young people as many of us had cars and learned mechanics as early as 16 which was the age I earned my first car.

Experimenting with Hot Rods, we learned how to get the most out of any engine, which proved valuable in flying a fighter.

I arrived in England and waited there to be a replacement for D-Day, getting a chance to fly with experienced combat pilots occasionally in mock "Dog Fights" This proved to be much more severe flying than had been allowed in the States.

We were flown into one of the first strips available and located a truck to try to find A-12. We searched for quite a while driving right past the Long Toms and Howitzer and some tanks. Tanks that were retreating back with badly-burned men. We also saw bodies, which appeared to be in the process of being sewed in bags.

We found what was to be A-12 where machinery was being used to level a field. There were dummy planes that were supposed to look like P-47s made of wire and cloth with a 55 gal. drum of what I supposed to be old oil under them. We found a location in a hedgerow and settled in by digging a foxhole. That was our introduction to combat.

There was a tent set up where we could get food and water and while we were waiting, and we could watch the Long Tom being fired by the Canadian troops that were in the area.

We were amazed to feel the concussion of the firing and could see the shell going out if we stood right behind the barrel.

We ate using "Mess Kits" and washed them afterward in garbage cans filled with disinfectant as there was a shortage of water.

I flew my first missions from A-12 as a wingman to Maj. Flavon, a gentle smooth pilot in whom I felt confident.

The most important flying was in the St. Lo area where we helped the infantry all we could, even spotting for "Time on Target" (TOT) as it was too "hot" with flack for the little L-5 liaison artillery spotter planes.

When we withdrew a short distance so the proximity shells would not get near us, we watched at least 75 artillery pieces all fire at once into St. Lo. It was a sight that I can not forget. I understand the Germans captured were in bad shape from this along with the bombing from the Eighth Air Force.

At night or in the evening we were exposed to occasional single plane bombing attacks and shellfire on the ground.

We were so close to the front lines at A-12, that we had to make our take-offs and landing pattern backward to stay on our friendly side and avoid being shot at.

I believe our mail delivery plane was actually shot down in forgetting this.

Our local gunners shot down a ME-109 that was strafing our field one evening.

When the German pilot was asked which airplane he would rather challenge, he said a P-38 as it was so easy to identify.

One time I was out in the field on the Latrine, when a FW-190 dropped a bomb quite close,

Pilot-Lt. R.L. Sallee and Co-pilot P. Troolin

attempting to put a hole in our runway. I just got dust on me and left what I was doing to a different time.

We had one other Latrine that was on the road between the operations tent and where our planes were parked. It was great sport to try to catch some one busy there, as it was just a plain box out in the open. This was and invitation to throw rocks at the unlucky person as we traveled on the way to our planes.

Some memories bother me and one was when searching for targets, which meant, anything that moved, I came across a bivouac, or obvious camp area with four soldiers walking down the road that was 90 degrees to my line of flight. It all happened so quickly that when I touched the trigger of my 85 caliber guns I was right on top of them as all four just disintegrated. It was not a good sight and made me realize what must be happening to those soldiers that tried to hide in the road ditches when we strafed the length of the them with the trigger held down.

I find, I cannot be sorry. I did not want to be there in the first place, fighting a war. The Germans started it and they were being carried along by a mad-man and they did not have the guts to get rid of this crazy person themselves. Someone had to do all this killing to get to him and see that he was put away forever.

The true hell that our infantry went through in the Battle of the Bulge is told accurately by Stephen Ambrose in *Citizen Soldiers* one of the only books that gave a little credit to the P-47 Thunderbolts.

We flew with wool shirts and this caused a little trouble with chaffing on the neck as rule number one for a fighter pilot is to keep your head turning to watch your tail for enemy aircraft. A silk or nylon scarf was the answer for this. I had a nylon piece of cargo chute that served me well. Later, my wife to be sent me a heavy silk scarf that served even better as it was warmer.

Dec. 1944, Changing the Magneto's, P-47. (Courtesy of Wm. T. Barr, Jr.)

Left to right: 377th Electrical Crew MOS 685 Everett Hawkinson and William T. Barr. (Courtesy of Wm. T. Barr, Jr.)

Jack J. Kellar and his P-51 - A9B-380 Fighter Squadron. (Courtesy of Jack J. Kellar)

British "Horsa" Troop Gliders-Normandy. (Courtesy of James T. Lee

April 1945, a Luftwaffe pilot landed his aircraft at Frankfurt, Germany and surrendered. (Courtesy of Pantoliano)

Taken at the Buchenwald Prison Camp in Weimar, Germany. (Courtesy of Pantoliano)

Veterans' Biographies

G.R. AMMERMAN enlisted in the USAAC May 8, 1941 and graduated from Air Mechanics School, Chanute Field in December 1941. He was crew chief on AT-6s at Maxwell Field until he volunteered for glider flying and completed glider pilot training in the class 42-19A at South Plains Army Flying School, Lubbock TX, Feb. 4, 1943 with the rank of flight officer.

Ammerman was assigned to the 436th TCG, 81st Sqdn. based at Membury in England and flew a British Horsa glider D-Day carrying 7,200 pounds of ammo to Normandy near St. Mere Eglise. On D-Day he worked with the 82nd Abn. Div. Ammerman made a combat landing behind enemy lines in Holland, Operation Market-Garden, carrying men of the 101st Abn. He carried men of the 17th Abn. across the Rhine at Wessel, Germany in Varsity. He completed service as first lieutenant and earned three Air Medals, the Dutch Orange Lanyard and the Presidential Unit Citation. He was discharged on April 1, 1946.

Ammerman married Jane L. Burke of Dugger, IN and they have one daughter and four sons. He earned the doctor of philosophy degree at Purdue University and worked as director of research for Libby McNeil and Libby 10 years and served on the staff and as department head of the Food Science Department at Mississippi State University for 21 years. He is a retired professor emeritus and resides in Aliceville, AL where he serves as an advisor to the Pickens County Commissioners.

CHARLES W. ANDERSON was drafted in April 1941 into the 28th Inf. Regt., 8th Inf. Div., Fort Jackson, SC. He transferred to the Aviation Cadets in July 1942 with Class 43-C. Commissioned March 20, 1943, at Pampa Field, TX. He did transition flying in C-47 at Bergstrom AFB, TX and was ordered to Alliance AFB, NE with the 80th TCS, 436th TCG in June 1943.

Moved to Laurinberg-Maxton AFB, NC in July 1943 for training including paratroop drop and glider towing. Went overseas in December 1943, losing an engine on first leg, delaying arrival in UK. Participated in all airborne missions in Europe in 1944 and 1945 from bases in Membury, England and Melun, France.

Decorated with Air Medal w/4 OLCs, AF Outstanding Unit Award, Presidential Unit Citation, American Campaign Medal, WWII Victory Medal, EAME Medal with Silver Star and two Bronze Stars.

Returned to the US and was separated in November 1945. He was recalled with ADC in June 1951; served as Detachment CO, Ground Observer Filter Center, Bismark, ND and returned to civilian life in March 1953.

Anderson is a graduate of University of Buffalo, NY, earning a BS in business/accounting. He worked for Remington Rand-Sperry Rand-Univac until retiring in 1978 at Blue Bell, PA. He is married to the former Dorothy Lee Osborne since 1946 and they have three children and three grandchildren.

JAMES M. "ANDY" ANDERSON JR., born June 26, 1920 in Alice, TX. He enlisted in the USAAC Jan. 8, 1942, Fort Sam Houston, TX and served in the following units:

February-December 1942 at Selfridge Field, MI with Recruit Det., Co. E, Plt. 3, Hangar 10; HQ&HQ Sqdn. 308th AB Gp.; and First Concentration Cmd. Det. December 1942, HQ 326th FG, Westover Field, MA; NY Air Defense Wg., NYC, TDY to attend Aircraft Recognition School in January 1943; HQ 362nd FG, Westover Field, MA, March 1943; and served with 379th FS, 362nd FG at Westover Field, MA; Bradley Field, CT; Groton AAB, CT; Mitchell Field, NY; and Camp Shanks, NJ.

Boarded *Queen Elizabeth* Nov. 21, 1943 and served Station 159 Wormingford, Essex, England; Station 412, Headcorn, Kent, England; A-12 Balleroy, Normandy, France; A-27 Aerodrome, Rennes-St. Jacques, Brittany, France; A-79 Aerodrome, Reims-Prosnes, Champagne, France; A-82 Aerodrome, Etain-Rouvres, Meuse, France.

November 1944, XIX Tactical Air Cmd. HQ (Adv.), Nancy France; Luxembourg City, Luxembourg;

Oberstein, Germany; Frankfurt, Germany; Bad Nauheim, Germany; Hersfeld, Germany; Erlangen, Bavaria. July 1945, HQ Ninth AF, Bad Kissingen, Germany. September 1945, 3rd Radio Sqdn. (Mobile) (Ground), Bad Kissingen, Germany; Staging Area, Le Havre, France; USS *West Point* to Norfolk, VA; Fort Sam Houston, TX.

TSgt. Anderson received honorable discharge Oct. 11, 1945. Awards include the Good Conduct Medal, PUC and EAME Theater Medal w/6 Battle Stars.

An unforgettable memory was visit to the German Death Camp at Buchenwald following liberation by units of 3rd Army. Stacks of naked, starved corpses and piles of ashes spoke loudly of Nazi inhumanity to fellow man.

Following the war he achieved bachelor of journalism degree from the University of Texas, and retired from Sentry Insurance in June 1992 as a career personnel manager. Married Betty Jean Pennington July 30, 1949 and they have two sons and five grandchildren. He is active with 362ND FG Assn. and serves as assistant secretary.

ROBERT D. ANDRUS, enlisted in USAAC in September 1942 and was called into service in March 1943. He went through college training at Shawnee, OK; went to cadet training at San Antonio; and pilot training at Parks Air College.

Graduated from ALOE Field, Victoria, TX and

assigned to Goldsboro, NC for P-47 training. Shipped out to France during Battle of the Bulge to the 368th Gp., 395th Sqdn. and flew 43 combat missions and stayed in occupation until March 1946.

Returned home in April 1946, married Audrey Moser in 1947 and they have three children and six grandchildren. He stayed in the USAFR and retired as lieutenant colonel.

JOSEPH C. ANTRIM, born Oct. 20, 1915, Columbus, OH. He was commissioned 2nd lieutenant, Ordnance Dept. upon graduation from ROTC training, Cornell University June 7, 1938. Spent 15 day tour active duty with Heavy Maint. Ord. Co., Fort Knox, KY, in July 1938.

On Oct. 12, 1940 he enrolled in Dept. of Commerce Civilian Pilot Training and completed in March 1941. Ordered to EAD Jan-Dec 1941 with 31st Ord. Co. Heavy Maint., Fort Benning, GA as shop officer; attended M4 AA Fire Control Director, Aberdeen Proving Ground, 1941; CO of 65th Ord. Ammunition Co., Fort Benning, GA, 1941-42.

In March 1942 transferred to Kelly Field, TX for pre-flight training; primary flight training at Spartan School of Aeronautics, Tulsa, OK; basic at Randolph Field, TX; and advanced at Ellington Field, TX. Graduated Class of 42-J and transferred to AC Res.

Assigned to 375th TCG, 58th Sqdn. upon completion of flight training at Warrensburg, MO; March 1943 formed cadre for 437th TCG and attended four week course at AAF School of applied Tactics, Orlando, FL; attended Camouflage School, March Field, CA, June-July 1943; Oxygen School, Randolph Field, TX, July 1943.

Assigned in October 1943 as 85th Sqdn. Ops. Officer, 437th TCG and moved to the ETO in January 1944 where he participated in the following campaigns: Normandy, Southern France, Northern France, Rome Arno, Rhineland, Central Europe and Ardennes. He flew 24 combat missions. Discharged with the rank of major.

JOHN M. BALOGA, enlisted in USAAC Aug. 29, 1942 and was fighter bomber pilot, P-47 Thunderbolt and flew 60 combat missions and 120 sorties in France and Germany and was support for General Patton's drive across France and Germany.

Received honorable discharge Oct. 22, 1945 with the rank first lieutenant. Awards include Air Offensive Europe, Northern France, Southern France, Normandy, Rhineland and Central Europe medals, Air Medal w/11 OLCs, EAME Theatre

Ribbon w/5 Battle Stars, one Overseas Service Star and Distinguished Unit Citation.

Earned BS degree at Lehigh University with Honors and worked for Allied Stores Corp. as operations mgr., West Side Vocational Tech High School as business mgr. and Penn State University, Wilkes Barre, as director business services. Retired Dec. 31, 1991.

Married 46 years to his late wife, F. Patricia (Gaj) and they have seven children: John, Stephen, Thomas, Patricia (infant deceased), David, Alice Mary, Joseph and 16 grandchildren.

He is a member of American Legion, DAV and Veterans of Foreign Wars.

WILLIAM T. BARR, born Feb. 19, 1924, Richmond, VA. Enlisted in USAAC Nov. 3, 1942 and awarded MOS 685 Aircraft Electrical Specialist and assigned to 377th FS, 362nd Gp. at Westover.

Served two years in Europe with 9th AF (P-47) in England, France and Germany. Discharged and joined the Reserve as staff sergeant in November 1945. Recalled 1950-51. Returned to active duty in May 1958 with 354th TAC Ftr. Wg. 9th AF, Myrtle Beach AFB, SC.

Retired May 1, 1984 as a chief master sergeant with 30 years active duty and 11 years reserve. He received 16 ribbons including the Meritorious Service Medal w/2 OLCs, AF Commendation Medal w/2 OLCs, DUC w/OLC and Master Missile Badge.

His most memorable experience was Omaha Beach and the heavy German shell fire in Normandy. He was the last enlisted WWII USAF Veteran to retire.

Married to former Nancy Miller and they have four children and two grandchildren. Retired to a farm at Rockville, VA.

ROY D. BARTLEY enlisted in the USAAC in July 1942 and was called up in January 1943 in San Antonio Aviation Center in Class 43-J. He was commissioned as 2nd lieutenant pilot in November at Aloe Field, Victoria, TX. Trained as P-47 pilot at Harding Field, Baton Rouge.

In May 1944, he joined 377th Sqdn., 362nd Gp. at Headcorn, Kent, England. Group transferred to strip A-12 in Normandy in July. On Aug. 4, on 33rd mission, plane was hit by ground fire and crash landed (unhurt). Was German POW in Stalag Luft 3 at Sagan, Silesia. In late January 1945, he transferred to Mooseburg, Germany camp and was liberated in late April.

Returned to Muncie, IN and married former Lois Mullins Barker in 1945. They divorced in 1965. He married the former Ursel Brown Sprong in 1971 and widowed in December 2000. Roy was a home builder until he retired.

WILLIS R. "BILL" BEALMEAR, enlisted in the USAAC July 23, 1940. Basic training was at Kelley and Brooks Fields in Texas. He attended Armament School at Lowry Field, Denver, CO on Jan. 1, 1941. After graduation he was kept on as an instructor, attaining the rank of staff sergeant.

In February 1943 he was transferred to Westover Field at Springfield, MA as a member of the newly formed 370th FG, 402nd FS with P-47s.

Sent overseas in January 1944, they were given P-38s and stationed at Andover, England with the 9th AF. He was promoted to armament inspector and tech sergeant. They moved to Normandy on July 23, 1944 at various strips throughout France, Belgium and Germany. While in Germany they were given P-51s.

After his discharge Sept. 30, 1945 at Fort Logan, Denver, CO, he became a captain on the Denver Fire Department and retired in July 1969.

LEONARD R. BENNETT entered service Jan. 5, 1943 at Santa Anna, CA, ordered to Nashville for classification at Maxwell Field and took preflight at Lakeland, FL, Courtland and Selma, AL, where he graduated with Class 43-K, then went to Venice, FL for P-47 training.

Landed at Liverpool, England April 30, 1944 and after more training at Atcham Field he was ordered to 10th FS, Lymington, England June 4. Flew his first mission June 8 to St. Lo, France and landed A-l0, France, June 25, 2nd wheels up landing on his 22nd mission and spent four months in hospital.

Rejoined 10th FS, Nov. 30, 1944, Toul, France. He flew total of 101 missions. Awarded DFC, Purple

Heart, Air Medal w/15 OLCs, Presidential Citation w/OLC, ETO, WWII Victory Medal, American Defense and French Croix de Guerre w/palm. Discharged with the rank first lieutenant.

Served with Air Reserve and Nebraska Air Guard and retired as lieutenant colonel with over 20 years service.

On Oct. 16, 1943, in Selma, AL, he married Gladys and they have one son, three daughters, 13 grandchildren and six great-grandchildren. He owned and managed a farm equipment sales and service business until retirement in 1982.

FRANK BERCHEK, a native of St. Louis, MO, he was a mechanic on C-47 and C-46 aircraft as a sergeant in the 94th TCS., 439th TCG. It was a honor to have served in the same squadron as Col. Charles H. Young, whose son authored the narrative of Troop Carrier in

Vol. XII No. 2 Spring 2002 issue of the *Ninth Flyer.*

Frank worked as a design engineer at Emerson Electric Co., St. Louis, from where he retired. Frank and his wife, Hilda, celebrated their 60th anniversary on Sept. 12, 2002. They have two sons, a daughter, three grandsons and a granddaughter. Frank and Hilda are active seniors who stay busy with church fish fry's and other senior activities. They enjoy being with their grandchildren. Frank builds remote control model boats and is a member of the St. Louis Admirals R/C Model Boat Club.

CARL B. BERNSON entered the Army on Sept. 8, 1942 in Spokane, WA. He was sent to Camp Robinson, AR for basic training and from there to Midwest Trade School in Bloomington, IL in October 1942. After

graduation in January 1943 he was sent to Langley Field, VA and entered the USAAC. He stayed at Olmstead Field, PA until sent to the ETO.

Landed in Liverpool, England in late June 1944, flew to Cherbourg, France with the HQ & HQ Sqdn. of the 302nd Transport Wg. in July 1944. They were transferred to Orly Field, Paris, France in August 1944 and assigned to A-46 Airstrip, a C-47 Transport Gp. (Goonibirds) outside of Versailles, France with the 9th AF.

Their group transported personnel and freight to all other airfields in Europe and England. They left A-46 after VE-Day in May 1945 to Kassel, Germany then to Frankfurt, Germany and to Y-80 Airfield near Wisebadden, a German airport on the River Rhine.

In their duties they were in a position to receive four battle stars to their ETO Ribbon (Northern France, Ardennes, Rhineland and Central Europe). He was discharged from the USAC as a sergeant on Jan. 15, 1946.

He was owner of a wholesale greenhouse-florist in Spokane, WA until he sold the business and retired in 1985. He is now 81 years old and he and his wife Ann love to travel and he enjoys playing golf.

ARCHIE E. BILLINGS, born May 6, 1922 in Edinboro, PA. Enlisted in USAAC in 1941 while in college at Edinboro State Teachers College where he graduated before entering active duty as Army Air Cadet on April 17, 1942.

He graduated with Class 44-B and commissioned 2nd lieutenant on Feb. 8, 1944 at Moore Field, TX. He was sent to Dale Mobry Replacement Depot, Det. Flt. J. Mobry Field, Tallahassee, FL.

After P-51 training he was assigned overseas Aug. 14, 1944 to the 363rd FG, 381st FS at Maupertus, France. On Aug. 22, the group moved to Azeville, France and three days later the unit was changed to a tactical recon. group. He asked for an assignment to fighter group. He was assigned to the 362nd FG 377th FS at Rennes, France, flying P-47s on Sept. 5, 1944. The fighter group was then moved to Reims, France on Sept. 18 in support of Gen. Patton's 3rd Army in the eastern France-Saarbrucken "Flak Ally" area. On Nov. 5 the fighter group moved to an airfield east of Etain (Meuse) France. He flew around 42 missions including some during the Battle of the Bulge.

His memorable experiences were three accidents in training - in one, a plane landed on his and the prop chewed up to his head piece.

He was KIA on Feb. 13, 1945 during an attack in the Motach area south of Luxembourg. Internment was at Luxembourg American Cemetery. His awards included the Air Medal w/5 OLCs and Purple Heart.

Survived by his parents, a sister and an older brother who was a staff sergeant in the 1000th Engrs. Treadway Bridge Co. in ETO.

THEODORE R. "TED" BLAIR, born Aug. 17, 1922 at Paia, Maui, HI and graduated Hunington Park High School in California. Enlisted in the USAAC as aviation cadet Sept. 21, 1942 with basic training at Sheppard Field, TX; preflight at San Antonio; primary at Corsicano, TX; BT-13 basic flying, Majors Field, Greenville, TX and AT-6 advance flying, Aloe Field, Victoria, TX. Graduated with Class 44-F as 2nd lieutenant June 27, 1944.

Departed Hampton Rhodes, VA on liberty ship and arrived Marseilles, France Jan. 1, 1945. In February 1945 he joined the 362nd FG, 379th FS, 9th AF and flew 25 missions in France and Germany. He was awarded the Air Medal w/4 Bronze Clusters, two Battle Stars and a PUC w/Bronze Cluster.

Returned to the USA aboard USS *General Morton* in September 1945 and was separated. He was recalled during the Korean War and stationed in Freishing, Germany, with 501st Tactical Control Gp., 604th Aircraft Control and Warning Sqdn. as radar controller, 1951-54, and retired with the rank of captain.

Returned to the USA and resided in Big Bear, CA, moved to Palmdale, CA and joined Convair Corp. then joined Lockheed Aeronautical Systems Co. until retirement in 1983. Ted passed away Sept. 6, 1990.

He and Phyllis were married Sept. 15, 1945 and had two children, Linda and Thomas, and one grandson, James.

CHET BORECK, born in Clifton, NJ, graduated from Clifton High School, attended University of Vermont, Fairleigh Dickinson College and holds a law degree from LaSalle Extension University. A licensed real estate broker, He was a P-47 pilot in the 377th Sqdn., 362nd FG in the 9th AF.

He flew 53 combat missions and was awarded the DFC by General Hoyt Vandenberg. The award was for extraordinary achievement in aerial flight against the enemy on April 8, 1945 near Eisenach, Germany.

Observing an enemy locomotive and five box cars that were loaded with ammunition, Lt. Boreck immediately dived to the attack, and in a brilliantly executed low-level bombing run, he destroyed the locomotive and box cars. Although his aircraft sustained severe battle damage in this action, he nevertheless engaged a ME-109 and severely damaged it; and while he was constantly subjected to enemy ground batteries, Lt. Boreck, by his superior airmanship and courage, returned his aircraft to base without incident. He was credited with downing three German fighter planes in combat.

Upon his release from the Air Force, Boreck organized the North Jersey Millwork Corp. and was a principal stockholder of that firm. He was also the executive vice president and general manager of the Glen Rock Lumber and Supply Corp. of Fairlawn, NJ, a major building material company serving customers in the United States and throughout the world.

"Chet" as he is known to his many associates, was also an active Lion member having served as secretary and president. He was also voted "Man of the Year" twice for his dedication to his fellow man and was also the founder of the Fairlawn Community Blood Bank and president for several years. He presently resides at 3 Wales Court, Forked River, NJ. He is still active in the US Coast Guard Auxiliary.

His wife Jo passed away seven years ago. He has a son, Robert Boreck, who resides in Hasbrouck Heights, NJ with his wife Nancy and daughter Andrea.

HENRY N. BOURQUIN, born March 4, 1923, Union City, NJ. He graduated pilot training in April 1944, went home on leave and married Hannah. He's a graduate of Rutgers University.

Served with the Ninth Air Force in the ETO with the 362nd FG, 379th FS as a pilot in P-47 Thunderbolt and completed 69

combat missions. Received the Air Medal w/13 clusters and Group Citation w/cluster.

Some of his memorable experiences included: when only one wheel came down for landing and flew in circles, rocked plane and flew upside down to shake wheel loose; saw target behind tall chimney, spun around and learned there were two chimneys and had to go through standing on one wing; lost pitot tube and followed another plane down runway; and arriving at Battle of Bulge and sky was blanketed with black and white puffs of flak – going through was scary.

He was on leave in Times Square, NYC when Japan surrendered. He was originally scheduled to go to Pacific Theater but rescheduled to Scott Field, IL as pilot and supply officer.

Eventually re-entered business world and retired as vice president of Turner Halsey Co. Inc., NYC Currently, as a retiree, he is a volunteer at McGuire AFB in New Jersey;

ROBERT V. BRULLE is from a small farm in Oordegem, Flanders Belgium, but grew up in Chicago, IL where the family settled after immigrating to America in 1929. Fortunately he received a 10 year citizenship requirement waver to become a pilot and received his wings and commission on Feb. 8, 1944. Assigned to the 9th AF,
366th FG he completed 70 P-47 combat missions, the most memorable occurring Jan. 1, 1945 when eight aircraft, just after take off, thwarted 60 German fighters from strafing their Belgium air strip.

Recently his book on the 366th titled *"Angels Zero,"* was published by the Smithsonian Institution Press. After the war he earned an advanced degree in aeronautical engineering, and had an adventure in aviation as a pilot, engineer, professor and entrepreneur which he's writing up as his next book.

Married to Margie Roth, mother of their four children who presented them with five grandchildren.

KEN BULLOCK was born in Winnipeg, Canada, June 2, 1921. He joined the USAAC on March 10, 1943; graduated from Foster Field, Victoria, TX, January 7th with Class 44-A. He was a test pilot at Wright-Patterson before being transferred overseas on Dec. 24, 1944.

Joined the 9th AF, 362nd FG, 378th FS. On April 12, 1945, he flew Red Four and became separated flying into a severe thunderstorm, was attacked by eight ME-109s over a German airfield - four broke left and four broke
right. Two bandits crossed in front of him. He fired a short burst from 80 degrees. When they came out the right side in front of him, one bandit was smoking. They lowered their landing gears, and he dove down, met them head-on, hit the smoking one first, then the wingman. They crashed on the airfield. Being overly enthusiastic, Bullock did two victory rolls over the German airfield, and in middle of his second roll was hit by AA, but landed back at the "home strip" in the rain. His crew chief "Zeke" was waiting for him. While taxiing back, with Zeke on the wing, they ran out of gas en route to the parking ramp. Minutes later, during the briefing, Ken learned that President Roosevelt had died, that same day. He received the Air Medal w/14 OLCs and the DUC in 1945.

Bullock has been a commercial flight instructor all his life and appeared on the History Channel in *Thunderbolts: Conquest Of The Reich*. Married 53 beautiful years to the former Dana Artrip, deceased May 11, 2000. He has two children, Mondie and Roger, and six grandchildren. Retired, he resides in Alexandria, VA and attends the annual air show at Andrews AFB, MD. He desires to build an ultralite and fly it to Osh Kosh!

PAUL L. CARLL, born in Elgin, Kansas July 1, 1920. Inducted into flying cadet program at Pittsburgh, PA, Dec. 8, 1941. Pilot Class 43-A, Craig Field, Selma, AL. Second lieutenant ORC, 0-795571 (AT-6). RTU Sarasota, FL (P-40). North Africa March 1943, assigned to 57th FG, 64th FS, British Western Desert AF, then 9th AF

(USA), then 12th AF. Flew in North African Campaign, Sicily, Italy, Yugoslavia, Southern France. Completed 114 combat missions (87 in P-40s and 27 in P-47s), three ME-109s shot down.

Returned to States in June 1944 and served with several developing procedure to knock out German V-1 and V-2 launch sites; Headquarters 1st AF, Mitchell Field, NY as head of Enlisted Personnel Section. Looked after Project R personnel in 1st AF. Was in charge of logistics for staging and transporting personnel transitions from European Theater to Far East Theater after Germany capitulated (those people going through 1st AF bases).

Separated from service in February 1946 with the rank of captain. He remained in ORC until resignation in October 1959. Awards include the DFC, Croix de Guerre w/Palm, Air Medal with several clusters, PUC w/3 clusters and other campaign medals.

Recalled in 1951 for Korea but was deferred as member of essential industry. Forty plus years career in chemical industry with The Lubrizol Corp., Cleveland, OH.

Married his lovely wife, Marian, June 6, 1944. They have two great sons and a beautiful daughter, all married. They have three grandsons and three granddaughters. Sixteen years of retirement have been rewarding. Marian and he enjoy good health and look forward to many more happy years together

J. ROBERT CAUSBIE, born July 23, 1920, Kauffman County, TX. He joined the USAC in mid-December 1941 and reported Jan. 19, 1942, Sheppard Field, Wichita Falls, TX. Assignments: March 10, 1942, School Squadron 42-7, Chanute Field, IL; April 1942 to Buffalo, NY, Curtis Wright, P-40 special 30 day course; May 1942 to Farming Dale, LI, 56th FG, 63rd FS and first to receive P-47, assistant crew chief on 12 and 13 aircraft received by Air Core.

Reported to 326th FG, 320th Sqdn. October 1942, Westover Field, MA, training crews (mechanics and pilots) for combat groups.

Assigned to 368th FG, 397th Sq. and sailed for ETO on Dec. 28, 1943 on USS *Argentina* luxury liner. Arrived Jan. 12, 1944 and assigned to 9th AF in England. Was first to be fully operational in France mid-June 1944. At end of combat had 237 missions and no aborts.

Most memorable day, Jan. 14, 1945, 12 plane mission - two did not take off, two aborts in flight, two returned and six downed by (40) FW-190. His plane, with 1st Lt. M.S. Bender, downed and became the only pilot to be a POW, none killed. Pilots assigned to his plane in combat were Marvin J. Rosvold, Joe R. Burney, M.S. Bender and Sid Horowitz. He crewed for Marvin J. Rosvold.

Discharged Oct. 19, 1945, Fort Sam Houston, San Antonio. Received Bronze Star for 100 missions, Good Conduct, ETO and five Battle Stars.

Married 52 years and has five daughters, eight grandchildren, and one great-granddaughter. Retired as a rural mail carrier and Weatherford Independent School District. Currently employed by Cotton-Bratton Funeral Home.

A. DAVID CHILDS, sworn in for aviation cadet training in May 1942. His wife, Peggy, pinned on his pilot's wings. Also awarded, were wings inscribed "Luke Field - P.T. Champions Class 44-B."

Several of this alphabetical 10 became Jug pilots at Harding Field, Baton Rouge; four joined the 377th FS, 362nd FG in Normandy, A-12.

November 17, 1944, on his 47th mission, both he and his plane were hit by 20mm ground fire. His chute opened at treetops and he was taken to Kaiserslautern hospital and had German doctor and nurses for 10 days, then moved to Stalag IV-B, where French doctor and medics and British NCOs (all POWs) gave Dave care and a future. Misery at Nurnberg Stalag IIID was followed by joy of Mooseburg Stalag VIIA liberation on April 29, 1945, with the 14th Armd. at the gate and a squadron of red-tipped P-47s orbiting overhead!'

American doctors and nurses in plastic and orthopedic wards at Dibble and Macornack military hospitals, get gratitude and praise for care given during those "overtime" years of WWII.

Awards include the DFC, Air Medal w/6 OLCs, Purple Heart, two Presidential Unit Citations, and Liberation of Normandy Medal (French 1994).

Graduated with honors in agricultural engineering and farmed for 40 years. He flew hundreds of hours studying Oregon's watersheds; a student of water's behavior with land. Got jump-start in 1944! "Seeing Europe Again: This Time With Peg" is the working title for their shared war stories. Those scenes, they've visited and revisited.

Children are Chris, named for squadron mate KIA October 1944, and Kathleen, because of two Irish great-grandmothers.

Grandson David is 16 and rides a 250 CC bike in 100 mile desert races, and occasionally chauffeurs grandfather to mountain headwaters.

BERNARD CIRANTINEO, born Jan. 15, 1922. Served with the 368th FG, Oct. 3, 1942 to Oct. 15, 1945. His memorable experience was crossing the Channel and landing in Normandy at St. Laurent Sur Mer. They left the LST during a big show of AA fire. He hesitated a moment and the loadmaster said, "Come on in, it's only up to your waist." The liar - it was up to his eyes. He saved himself by dancing on his tippy toes. On the beach, they rested for a moment, then up to the cliff to a farmer's field. In the morning they saw soldiers in foxholes around them, one guy loudly proclaimed, "The war is over, the Air Force is here." They then went to Strip 3 and waited for it to be completed. A week later, their planes would arrive for fuel and ammo, fly and bomb all day and return to England before nightfall. He was an armorer on a P-47, number D3F, on Marvin Rosvold's plane. The pilot of his second plane was Sid Horowitz.

Discharged with the rank of corporal. His awards include the ETO Ribbon w/6 Battle Stars and the Distinguished Unit Citation.

He married Nancy Sanfilippo on Sept. 27, 1947 and they have two children, Roberta and Keith. Bernard had a successful 34-year career as a salesman with Bowman Distribution Co., Barnes Group, Inc.

RICHARD AUSTIN CLINE enlisted in the Air Corps in January 1942, and at 24 was commissioned a lieutenant-colonel. He was born in Miami, FL, and was a graduate of Miami Senior High School's class of 1938. He was attending Maryville College, Maryville, TN when he enlisted.

Cline was a member of "Mogin's Maulers," Ninth Air Force. During the European campaign, he led his P-47 Thunderbolt group daily against retreating Nazi convoys. The French government decorated him with the Croix de Guerre with Vermilion Star in July 1945. He also received the DFC, Silver Star, and Air Medal w/ 19 clusters. Cline was a veteran of 118 missions.

Richard married Julia Bryant, had one daughter Kathleen Cline Saunders, and two grandsons, Lee and Richard Saunders. Lt. Col. Cline was killed Dec. 28, 1947 in an airplane crash over Honshu, Japan. He had been stationed in Korea, as director of training.

JAMES B. COHEA, born in Gisela, AZ. He enlisted January 13 in Arizona and served with the 367th, 9th AF in campaigns and battles in Air Offensive Europe, Normandy, Northern France, Ardennes, Central Europe and Rhineland.

Discharged in September 1945 with the rank of master sergeant, his awards included the Good Conduct Medal, EAME Campaign Medal and DUB w/OLC.

Attended Northern Arizona University for AB degree, 1941 and master degree at Northern Colorado University in 1952. He was a cattle rancher and school principal in Young, AZ; moved to Phoenix in 1961 where he retired as a teacher in 1979. He passed away Feb. 22, 2001.

Married Susan Devenney on June 12, 1953 and had daughter Margaret who is with the U.S. Dept. of State, Berlin, Germany.

RICHARD E. CONE enlisted in the USAAC Cadets, May 20, 1942 with Class 43-B. Commissioned Feb. 6, 1943, at Luke Field, Phoenix, AZ and assigned to Sarasota, FL for training. Transferred May 20th to 9th AF, North  Africa with Combat Operations from Cairo, Kairouan to Cape Bon, Tunisia.

Flew with the 99th all black fighter squadron on their first mission over Pantelleria. Downed by enemy gun fire on July 8, 1943 escorting light bombers near Sciacca, Sicily. Chuted down to the sea and was taken prisoner. He was operated on by a civilian doctor. Released by US troops July 20, 1943 and returned to US hospital on Oct. 1, 1943. After many hospital stays he was discharged Jan. 22, 1947, Camp Beal, CA.

Decorated with EAME Medal, WWII Victory Medal, American Campaign Medal and Order of the Purple Heart.

Married Lois N. Baughman and they have two children, five grandchildren, and seven great-grandchildren. Married second, Mary C. Draper and has two stepchildren.

Worked 28 years as a design engineer for NCR Corp. and is now retired.

WENDALL CONNER, born March 7, 1920, De Land, IL. Enlisted in the service Jan. 3, 1942 and commissioned 2nd lieutenant in 1943.

Military Experience: Troop Carriers, ground officer, 16 PCSs in 22 months, WWII, ETO, 9th AF, six Battle Stars, 1943-45. He served with the 362nd Ftr. BG and was injured during the Battle of the Bulge. He volunteered for Korean War and Vietnam War, served 2-1/2 years in Morocco and in Iceland in 1963.

Retired with the rank of lieutenant colonel at Keesler AFB, MS in May 1970.

He and Catherine were married in 1942 and have one daughter, Christie. He pushed wheel chairs for years at Keesler Medical Center and was a Red Cross volunteer. He is now totally retired because of his heart condition.

FRANCIS A. CONNOR JR., a graduate of Melrose High School and Roanoke College, Salem, VA, he enlisted for air cadet training. Lt. Connor served with the 362nd FG. A former employee of the State Street Trust Co., he flew on more than 20 missions escorting bombers, dive bombing and strafing enemy airfields and railway yards.

He was all set to be baptized in the English Channel when his P-47 Thunderbolt fighter, named *Ann Noel,* ran out of gas after an over-extended flight to Brunswick, Germany, but an 80 mph tail wind, radio directions from the RAF Sea Rescue Service, and a sudden hole in the clouds helped him to make an emergency beach landing.

His motor conked out when he was still three miles out over the Channel. Over the Zuider Zee, still 100 miles from the English Coast, he decided to fly as near the English side as possible and hoped to get picked up by Air Sea Rescue. He nursed his plane along at 210 mph, stretching out the gas. That was the longest half-hour of his life.

Francis passed away Oct. 17, 2002. He is survived by his wife Ann; two daughters, Cheryl Perry and Noell Heckman; two sons, Roderick and Francis III; and many, many grandchildren.

MAYNARD L. COWLES, born in 1922 to Austin and Clara in southern Michigan and joined the USAAC in January 1943. He graduated from Aviation Cadets flying schools, received his commission as 2nd lieutenant, and completed P-47 Fighter School in August 1944.

On Oct. 7, 1944, he joined the 362nd FG, 378th FS of the 9th AF, stationed in Prosnes, France. On Nov. 4, 1944, the 362nd moved to Etain, France, where the fighter group stayed until April 1945.

Maynard made the ultimate sacrifice for his country on March 3, 1945, during mission #417, a bombing run on a railroad bridge in Irlich, Germany. He is buried at the Lorraine American Cemetery, operated by the American Battle Monuments Commission, in St. Avold, France, east of Metz, near the German border.

He received the Air Medal w/5 OLCs and the Purple Heart.

JOHN P. "JIM" CROW, born Dec. 31, 1921, Fort Payne, Dekalb County, AL. He graduated Auburn University with BS civil engineering degree in 1942. Entered OCS at Fort Belvoir, VA in February 1943 and was commissioned 2nd lieutenant, Corp of Engineers.

Transferred to Air Corps as Student Pilot Class 44-D Hawthorne School of Aeronautics, Orangeburg,

SC. Took his basic training at Shaw Field, Sumter, SC; advanced at Craig Field, Selma, AL; Gunnery, Eglin Field, FL; Basic P-47, Richmond, VA; P-47 Gunnery, Willington, NC.

Sail to England on *Aquitania* in October 1944 and joined the 48th FG, 492nd FG at St. Tround, Bel., Nov. 18, 1944. He flew six missions: Julich, Duren, Auchen. He was shot down on 7th mission, Battle of Bulge, Dec. 24, 1944. Strafed German vehicles near St. Vith that were out of fuel and followed them too far, he came up and squadron had formed and departed area. Saw three P-47s in distance and proceeded to join up when two FW-190s dropped right in his gun sights attacking the two lead P-47s. Crow latched on to one and followed him on down to deck with many hits, but couldn't confirm kill. He didn't know that two other FW-190s were on his tail. Stayed on deck at 100 feet full throttle until ridge with trees came up - as he hit top of trees a 20mm hit oil gauge in cockpit and he jettisoned canopy, pulled up and jumped at low altitude. Chute opened and he hit ground. Ground fire knocked one of FW-190s down. Friendly Belgiums took him to American troops and he was back at St. Tround about midnite. His roommates were sadly drinking their last bottle of Calvert Reserve that they were saving for Christmas.

Flew total of 45 missions. Sailed out of France and headed to South China Seas when they were re-routed to Boston, USA and resigned from Air Force with the rank 1st lieutenant. Awards include the Purple Heart, Air Medal w/5 clusters, DFC and Presidential Citation.

Obtained BA degree in civil engineering, Auburn University and spent 57 years in construction engineering, steel fabrication, real estate development and owner of Builders Supply Co., Inc., Fort Payne, AL.

He and wife Betty have three children, seven grandchildren and two great-grandchildren.

WILLIAM ROSS CUNNINGHAM, born March 26, 1923, Indianapolis, IN. He joined USAAC in 1942 and was a fighter pilot in the ETO during WWII. Served with 9th AF, 362nd FG, 379th FS and flew 29 missions in P-47 Thunderbolts. Cunningham was discharged in September 1945.

Enlisted in the Indiana National Guard in 1946, served active duty during Korean War, flew P-51s with Air Defense Command. Joined USAFR, Carswell Air Base, TX in 1961, flew C-124 with Military Transport Command (MAC) during Vietnam War.

LTC Cunningham retired in 1969. His awards include Command Pilot, DFC, Air Medal w/2 OLCs, Purple Heart, ETO Ribbon w/ 3 Bronze Stars and 10 awards for Korean and Vietnam Wars.

Civilian career as owner of a construction company. He married the former Peggy S. Yoder in 1948 and they have four children, 14 grandchildren and two great-grandchildren.

HOWARD J. CURRAN, born March 27, 1918, Pratt, KS. He joined the USAAF July 15, 1941 at Fort Riley, KS. Completed basic training at Jefferson Barracks, MO, September 1941 and Aircraft Armament Technical School, January 1942, Lowry Field, Denver, CO. He entered Aviation Cadet Program in September 1942, Southeast Training Command, Maxwell Field, AL and graduated from single engine pilot training, Class 1943, May 28, 1943, Spence Field, GA. Completed Fighter Pilot Training (RTU) in P-39s, Venice, FL, June-September 1943.

From October 1943 to February 1944 he was assigned to 405th FBG, 510th FS at Walterboro, SC for combat training in P-47 Thunderbolts prior to joining the 9th AF in the ETO.

In March 1944, the 405th FBG deployed to Christchurch, England, 9th AF and ETO; July 1944, they deployed to Fighter Strip #8, Normandy, France near St. Mere Elise; Sept. 12, 1944, on his 95th combat mission in P-47s, he was shot down and forced to bail out over German occupied France near Pont-A-Mousson (midway between Metz and Nancy on the Moselle River east of Paris). After six days of being an "evadee" and being aided by the local French people which prevented his capture by the Germans, he was liberated by advancing American Infantry. Sept. 18, 1944 to December 1944, in accordance with the existing military policy on evadee's, he was returned to US 9th AF control, duly processed and returned to the States for leave, R&R and re-assignment.

Memorable Experience: "I was shot down on Sept. 12, 1944 while flying my 95th mission, which was also the first mission for the 510th Sqdn., from our base at St. Dizier.

"During the afternoon on a sunny French day, I was in the company of my French benefactor, Francois Lertex, a young Frenchman who had been active in the French resistance and was still risking his life by helping me evade capture by the Germans.

"For the past few days the Germans to the east and the Americans to the west had been having an artillery duel and we had become so accustomed to it that we could identify the shells passing overhead by the sound.

"We were enjoying the lovely September afternoon in the stone walled courtyard behind the house where I was being hidden when a "short round" from the Americans fell in the courtyard near us luckily it fell just beyond us and the concussion and shrapnel from the exploding shell fragmented into the stone wall. Later we determined that it exploded less than 20 feet away from us.

"The moral of this experience is that except for 'the luck of the Irish' my flying career would have ended in a French courtyard by friendly artillery. Francois Lertex is still living and resides in Nancy, France."

From August 1946-June 1948, TDY, jet pilot training Williams Field, AZ in F-80 jet fighters; June-December 1948 stationed at Furstenfeldbruk, Germany with 6th FG; February 1949-June 1950, 1st FG, March AFB, CA, F-86s; July 1950-September 1951, Korea, assigned to the 51st FG, 16th FS, 5th AF and flew 105 combat missions in F-80s, jet fighter aircraft; October 1951-March 1952, assigned to 20th FG, Langley AFB, VA.

From April 1952 to September 1957 he was a flight test acceptance pilot, Republic Aviation Corp., Farmingdale, Long Island, NY; September 1957-October 1959, flight test officer, Chateauroux AFB, France; December 1959 to October 1961, McChord AFB, WA, data processing. Maj. Curran retired from the USAF Nov. 1, 1961. His combat decorations include DFC w/3 clusters, Air Medal w/24 clusters and Purple Heart.

He processed and delivered mail in Tacoma, WA from January 1962 to retirement in March 1983.

HARRY DAHLHEIMER, entered USAAC in February 1943, completed radio and aerial gunnery schools. Promoted to tech sergeant and assigned to a B-26 crew at Barksdale Field. With pilot, Benjamin F. Courtright, and copilot, Robert Finn, ferried a B-26 to England via Brazil, Ascension Island and North Africa. Assigned to 344th   BG 496th Sqdn. at Bishop's Stortford. Flew 68 missions, including D-Day mission. Moved to a base in France (Pontoise) in September 1944.

Rotated back to States and entered pilot training as aviation student in March 1945. Discharged on "points" in July 1945, his awards include the Air Medal w/12 OLCs and four Battle Stars.

After discharge he returned to college and earned BS and MA degrees at Wayne State University. He taught social studies in Detroit Public Schools and became a textbook editor in NYC. He earned PhD in history from University of Iowa, became a professor of history (1969) at State University of New York, College at Cortland. He is currently professor emeritus at Cortland College and chairman of B-26 Archive Advisory Council at Akron University.

ROBERT L. DAINS, enlisted as an aviation cadet in the USAAC June 30, 1942 and reported to Cadet Classification Center, Kelly Field, Sept. 10, 1942. Classified as a navigator, he took preflight at Ellington Field. Graduated from Hondo, TX, July 15, 1943 in Class 43-10-2 as a second lieutenant and assigned to Troop Carrier.

Arrived in England, via the southern route, on April 19, 1944. He partici-   pated in the D-day Invasion of Normandy with the 439th TCG. In July 1944 he volunteered to transfer to B-26s and was assigned to the 322nd BG. The group moved to Beauvais, France, September 1944. Then to Belgium on April 1, 1945. Assigned to B-17s, he flew Photo Recon. from Thurleigh England in June 1945.

In October 1945 he returned to the States and was discharged in March 1946 as a first lieutenant. He was awarded the Air Medal w/6 OLCs, five Battle Stars and Distinguished Unit Citation.

Robert married a British Army nurse he met in Belgium. They have four children and six grandchildren. He worked as a Cartographer for 32 years with the USAF/Dept. of Defense until retirement in March 1978.

RAY V. D'AVILA, Master Sergeant, USAF (Ret.) Dallas, TX, born Nov. 17, 1919. Assigned to 17th BG, 95th Sqdn., Gunnery Class 42-B. August 1941. Patrolled Gulf and Atlantic for subs in B-25. Transferred to Barksdale AFB to form 319th BG, 439th Sqdn. with B-26 Marauder, 12 weeks.

Flew aircraft over northern route for invasion of North Africa, was shot down on first mission and rescued by our fighter escort. First tour, 40 missions with 12th AF and second tour, 25 missions with 387th BG, 557th BS, 9th AF replacement crew during the Battle of the Bulge.

War ended and he returned to States. His awards include Air Medal, two Silver and two Bronze OLCs. He retired from the Air Force in November 1979.

Married Rosemary Braun in January 1952; they have three children and three grandchildren. He is a charter life member of 9th Air Force Association, life member AFA and member B-26 Marauder Historical Society. He now volunteers with AFA.

STANLEY J. DAVIS, Staff Sergeant, born in Ames, New York in 1922. He attended aeronautical schools in Chicago, IL and St. Louis, MO. Stan joined the unit at Tampa, FL when it was the 337th FG and moved with the outfit several times until Col. Ferguson formed the 405th Group in Walterboro, SC with the 510th as one of the three squadrons.

When the 405th shipped to the European Theater in February 1944, Stan was crew chief on a new P-47. Sgt. E. Marshall was assistant crew chief and Cpl. Ray Rappold was armorer. Their ship was piloted, at various times, by Marvin Leinweber, James Peletier, Harry Sanders and James Walton.

During his tour of duty, Davis participated in the Air Offensive Europe, Ardennes, Central Europe, Normandy, Northern France and Rhineland campaigns.

In 1945, Stan was relieved from active duty. His awards include the American Service Medal, Presidential Unit Citation, EAME Service Medal and Good Conduct Medal.

In 1948 he married Esther Jones in Morrisville, NY. Stan engaged in a number of occupations: farm equipment, dairy farming, beef cattle and school bus driving. Esther was a school teacher. They are both retired now and living in Florida.

ARTHUR C. DEROCHER, graduated from Avon High School in June 1936. In July he joined the Civilian Conservation Corps until April 1939. Things were looking bad in Europe so in September 1940 he joined the USAAC. Stationed at Westover Field until September 1941 when shipped to Newfoundland. They were looking for cooks so he signed up.

Returned to the States in December 1942 and was stationed at Grenier Field until March 1943 when he was assigned to the 378th FS of 362nd FG After training at different bases they shipped out of New York on the *Queen Elizabeth* for England where he flew missions with the 8th AF until D-day.

Memorable experiences include having his picture made with Joan Blondell; watching the P-47s getting ready to go on missions; sleeping in dug-outs in the ground at Omaha Beach and being strafed every night by Midnite Charlie.

He has lived in Florida since December 1984.

BENJAMIN J. DONTZIN, was born Oct. 18, 1920 in the Ukraine and in 1922 his family came to Manhattan. In 1942 Ben graduated from Cornell University and enlisted in the USAF.

Called to active duty April 29, 1943, Ben was attached to the 397th BG of the 9th AF. He flew 70 missions in the ETO and was awarded the French Croix de Guerre w/SS, the DFC, Air Medal w/14 OLCs, American Campaign Medal, EAME Medal and the

DUB. Capt. Dontzin left active duty March 3, 1946.

He farmed in New Jersey and served on the local school board.

Ben passed away March 11, 1997 and his ashes are interred at Arlington. He is survived by his wife Nancy, four daughters: Pat and Katie Campbell, Anne and Mary Dontzin, and two granddaughters, Kate and Betsy Randolph.

WAYNE EDWARD DOWNING, born 1919 in Ute, IA. Degrees were earned at Arizona University (BS in 1958) and Maine University (MEd. in 1963). He volunteered for the Aviation Cadet Program. Assignments: 1942-43, received commission and pilot wings, USAAF Class 42-F; 84th BG, Hunter Field, GA; 85th BG, Waycross, GA; Army maneuvers in Tennessee; 46th BG(L), Will Rogers, OK; and 30th Recon Sqdn. at Northern Field, TN.

From 1943-45, he flew 86 combat missions from England and France with the 2911 BS(L) and 416th BG; 1946-49 assigned to Aircraft Maintenance Officer School at Chanute Field, IL, then to Central and South Pacific to participate in Search and Recovery of "Body Bones, Bombs and Aircraft crashes" not yet recovered from WWII with USS LST-711 as cruise HQ; 1949-50, 27th FW, Bergstrom AFB, TX; 1951-52, completed engineering, armament and radiological courses at Minnesota University, MN, Fairchild AFB, WA, Edgewood Arsenal, MD, Lowry AFB, CO and flew the Tumbler-Snapper Atomic Tests in Nevada.

From 1952-53 assigned to new Jet Bomber Program and completed Jet Navigator, Air Radar Operator, Bombardier, and Air Gunner schools at Ellington AFB, TX, Mather AFB, CA and Davis-Monthan AFB, AZ; and received the respective USAF aeronautical ratings; 1953-59, 43d BG, Davis-Monthan AFB, AZ with Cold War mission TDYs to England, North Africa, Alaska and Guam; 1959-63, 4038th Strategic Wing, Dow AFB, ME with Cold War Airborne Alert missions to Russia's early warning net locations.

Awards include DFC, 17 Air Medals, six ETO Battle Stars, and two PUCs.

From 1963-98 he taught mathematics courses in high school and community college. In summer recesses worked with NATO country Military Reserve Officers in Europe. Completed all the levels of US Civil Air Patrol Search and Rescue training and flew search missions in mountains and desert of US Southwest. In 1982 he taught mathematics to sailors of the USN's Independence Battle Group operating in the Indian Ocean and the Arabian Sea based on USN's DDG-2 *C.F. Adams;* 1991-99 he did accounting work with Keyes Motor Co. of Van Nuys, CA.

He is married to Norma Raley, a US Army nurse during WWII. They have a daughter Nancy and granddaughter Sara.

J. FRANK EHRMAN, born June 21, 1924, Howard County, IN. Inducted into the USAAF on March 3, 1943 and reported to Ft. Benjamin Harrison, Indianapolis, IN. Attended Engineering and Operations at Colorado A&M College, Fort Collins, CO. After training, was assigned to HQ 50th TCW at Pope Field, NC.

Went to England aboard the *Queen Mary* and assigned to the A-1 Personnel Section for the balance of his military service at Cottesmore, Bottesford and Exeter, England. The 439th, 440th, 441st and 442nd TC groups were under our jurisdiction and our outfits participated in Normandy, Northern France, Rhineland, Southern France, Central Europe and Ardennes, spending time at Le Mans, and Chartres, France until V-E Day. Returned to the US and was discharged Oct. 17, 1945.

Attended Kokomo Business College, accounting course. Joined Chrysler Corp. in 1948 and attended Indiana University, Indianapolis campus in personnel management. Employed for 31 years after working at three plants in Indiana before retiring in 1979 as a personnel executive in the Human Resources Dept.

Married Nina Jean Morrison in 1946 and have two children, two grandchildren and three great-grandchildren. Returned to England and France in 1987 along with seven other couples to re-trace their WWII footsteps.

Since 1956, he has been secretary treasurer, editor of *Wingtips Newsletter,* Historian and Reunion Organizer for HQ 50th TCW Assn. where they have held reunions every two years in various cities throughout the USA.

Also employed by the Indiana Department of Revenue for six years as operations manager of the Mailing Department, then worked in maintenance and landscaping for condominium couples where we live and was on the Board of Managers for nine years before finally retiring to spend winters in Florida.

PHILL G. EMERT enlisted in USAAC in June 1941, Portland, OR. He graduated as a sergeant gun mechanic and entered Aviation Cadet School in September 1942 with Class 43-E and commissioned second lieutenant in August 1943 at Albany.

His military assignment was with the 313th TCG, 47th TCS and the 4th TC Pathfinder Sqdn. (Prov.) with the 9th AAF based in England and France. He was first pilot on C-46 and C-47 transports participating in glider tows, paradrops and resupply missions. His total flying time was approximately 1,000 hours.

Phill received the Air Medal, Good Conduct Medal, American Defense Service Medal and the EAME Campaign Medal w/6 BSs.

His battle campaigns were Normandy, Southern France, Northern France, Rhineland, Ardennes and Central Europe. 1st Lt. Emert returned to the States in July 1945 and was sworn into the USAAFR on Sept. 6, 1945. He put on his "Ruptured Duck" patch/lapel button and walked out the gate as a civilian.

Phill was a farmer-rancher and married to former Barbara Follett. They have four children: Phill Jr., Robert, Delores Spor and Connie McMillin; 10 grandchildren and 9 great-grandchildren. Both Phill and Barbara are deceased. *Submitted by Patricia Pettyjohn.*

ARTHUR E. EXON, was born in Geddes, SD in 1916. There he was educated, taught school and served as principal of the Fairfax Junior High, 1938-42.

In March 1942 he entered pilot training, was rated pilot in November 1942 and joined the 57th FG, 64th FS in North Africa in January 1943. By July of that year he was promoted to first lieutenant and assigned as squadron commander.

He flew 134 combat missions (dive bombing, strafing, bomber escort and aerial combat) in P-40s and P-47s in North Africa, Malta, Sicily, Italy and Corsica. He was a POW in Germany (Luft III), April 1944-April 1945.

A memorable experience for him was flying "Top Cover" for a flight of 34 P-40s that had been assigned to a mission over Cape Bonn Peninsula in North Africa on April 18, 1943. It was Palm Sunday when British Intelligence obtained information that Germans were trying to evacuate North Africa by air or other means available. When he arrived at Cape Bonn, he noticed 100 or more German airplanes flying in "V" or "Vs" right on the water. The 57th Fighter Group and others attacked the German planes and shot down 75. The Germans, over their radio, claimed 76 planes were destroyed. Exon shot down one Mig-109 and got a "probable" on the second 109.

Exon was discharged May 1, 1969. After the war, he continued his Air Force service with distinction in the fields of operations, logistics, A/C maintenance and retired as director, Defense Contract Administrative Service, May 1, 1969.

BG Exon's decorations include the Distinguished Service Cross, two Legion of Merits, DFC, Air Medal w/15 OLCs, the British DFC and the French Croix de Guerre w/Palm and Star.

He was married June 19, 1945, and has two sons. His wife, Scotty, passed away in 1987. After retiring in 1969, he became a "gentleman farmer," managing 4,500 acres of permanent crop in central California. He was president of a general partner company overseeing and managing the detail of farming and harvesting.

Today, he is fully retired and living at Air Force Village West in Riverside, California, with his wife, Eunice, who he married in 1993.

RUSSELL FAIRBANKS, born Sept. 12, 1921, Sicily Island, LA. At Louisiana State University he flew J-3 Cub and WACO UPF-7 in the CPTP. Called to active duty in January 1942, took pilot training in

Southeastern Training Command, graduating at Napier Field, Dothan, AL, Dec. 13, 1942, Class 42-K.

Trained on P-39s at various fields in Florida and Georgia; became engaged to future wife, Billie Sapp, Fort Myers, FL; and trained on P-39s and P-47s at Walterboro, SC.

Boarded the *Normandy* on March 13, 1944 with destination England. After Atcham combat training, he was assigned to the 377th FS, 362nd FG. The group moved to Caen sector, France, A-12 airstrip in July 1944 and as part of XIXth TAC, supported Gen. Patton's Third Army. Following Gen. Patton required several moves to other airstrips during Russell's tour.

He flew 90 missions receiving flak damage on 50 of them. Missions varied from 45 min. to over four hours. Missions included fighter sweeps, bomber escort, beach patrol, armed recces, dive bombing and strafing, and front line support. His group received the DUC w/2 OLCs for destroying German naval vessels in waters of Brest Harbor and dam busting. Russell was awarded two DFCs, 16 Air Medals, and the EAME Ribbon w/5 BSS.

Missions fresh in his memory are a Glide bombing mission on a gun pit under an 800 foot overcast at Brest in which his E4-0 took a 40mm in left elevator/stabilizer, nose flipped down and recovery made at tree-top level; close one with a head-on with a Me-109; and the intense, accurate mg 20mm and 40mm highly visible flak on a late, hazy afternoon over Saarbrucken, exploding ammo trains. He returned to the Big PX in April 1945 on the *Normandy,* married Billie who bore him two daughters, Autumn and Debra. From May 1945 to retirement in September 1962, his assignments included the Canal Zone (P-38s, P-47Ns); P-51s Ground Attack School, St. Petersburg, FL; T-6 Instructor's School and instructor at Perrin Field, TX; 3-year tour in England; Logistics in 376th and 19th BWs; a year at Sondrestrom AFB, Greenland, Logistics with the 4050th Air Refueling Wing, Westover, MA where he retired.

Russell received teaching certificate at Northeast Louisiana University and taught at Rosepine High School, LA for 30 years retiring in 1995. Billie, his love of 57 years of marriage, died in 2002. He feels blessed with a loving family that includes two grandsons, two granddaughters, and two great-grandchildren.

DR. JAMES FALL, born April 27, 1923 in rural Fulton County, IN, son of a WWI Air Force veteran. Volunteered for Air Corps July 1, 1942 with pre-flight at San Antonio, TX; primary flight training Victory Field, Vernon, TX; basic Enid Army Air Base, Enid, OK. Graduated from advanced with Class 43-J, Nov. 3, 1943, Foster Field, Victoria, TX. After few hours flying P-40s from Foster he was assigned Perry AFB, Perry, FL for P-47 transition.

On April 11, 1944 Lt. Fall joined the 391st FS, 366th FG, 9th AF, stationed Thruxton, England. On ground support mission June 10, 1944, during 21st mission with Holt's Hun Hunters, Fall's P-47 was terminally damaged by flak and he bailed out of flaming Thunderbolt near Rosel, France (unfortunately on unfriendly side of front lines). Although Lt. Fall landed within 350 yards of Canadian troops, he was captured by SS of 12th Hitlerjugend Panzerdivision and held POW at Dulag Luft, Stalag Luft III, Moosburg VIIA. He was liberated April 29, 1945 by 14th Armd. Div., Gen. Patton's 3rd Army.

With his mental image of fighter pilots somewhat tarnished by POW encounter, Fall returned to civilian life at termination of WWII, graduated from Indiana University School of Dentistry in 1950 and practiced general dentistry at Marion, IN until sudden loss of vision forced retirement in 2001.

Fall married his high school sweetheart, Ethel Mae Swank, in 1945. They have three children: Jo Ellen, Mark and Janet. Mark has their three grandchildren: Gina, John and Rob.

PAUL E. FAST, Tech Sergeant, was drafted into Army in August 1942 and sent to Sheppard Field, TX to learn aircraft maintenance. Specialty 750, he won Carbine Sharpshooter in September 1943.

Participated in battles and campaigns in Air Offensive Europe, Normandy, Northern France, Rhineland and Central Europe. Assigned to 394th BG,

5843rd BS, he was crew chief on a B-26 Martin Marauder, *Ish-Tak-Ha-Ba*. He flew 137 missions with bomb load of two tons   of bombs. The *Ish-Tak-Ha-Ba*, the oldest plane in unit, carried two crews safely through their tours of duty.

Sleepy Eye, MN was the hometown of pilot, Capt. Marter Harter who was KIA flying as lead aircraft on a mission in another aircraft. Anyone knowing anything about his family, please contact me. He was married and had children.

Paul's awards include Bronze Star, DUB w/7 OLCs and Good Conduct Medal.

DONALD J. FISHER from Passaic, NJ enlisted in the USAAC in August 1942. Basic training was at Fort Dix, NJ; Aircraft Engine Mechanic School at Keesler Air Field, MS; and from there to Willow Run, MI to become a crew member on a newly built B-24. The plane operated in the Florida area.

After further schooling in Fort Myers and Orlando, he went to the 423rd Night Fighter Sqdn. in September 1943. Locations were Orlando, FL, Kern County in California, Chormydown and Chalgrove, England. They were redesignated to the 155th Photo Rec. Sq. on June 22, 1944. The planes were A-20 Havocs. The 155th was awarded the PUC w/cluster.

Donald was a commercial draftsman and an amateur photographer. He passed away Dec. 7, 1967. *Submitted by his brother, Clifford R. Fisher.*

EVERETT "BILL" FISHER, born on Sept. 23, 1917, was a graduate of Milwaukee High School, former of Pacific University, and was driver of first aid car of Portland Fire Bureau before entering USAAF and serving in WWII

In high school he was a football star and captain of the boxing team. He served in the European Theatre and flew over 100 missions. He became one of the "Morgin's Maulers."

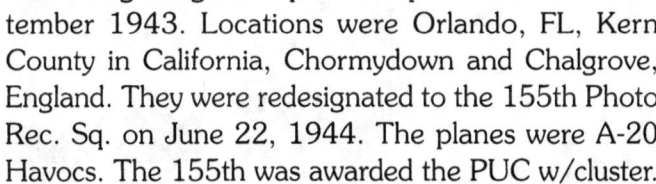

He was married to Shirley Jane Giltner on Dec. 23, 1940. *Submitted by his cousin, Diana Hyndman.*

JAMES FLINCHUM, born Oct. 15, 1923 in Willis, VA and he enlisted in the USAAC on March 10, 1943 before being sent to Crash & Rescue School at Lake Pontchartrain, near New Orleans, LA. He was then ordered to Camp Kilmer, NJ to pick up the USS *Monteray* and landed in   Liverpool. When he reached Boxted Air Base, he became a part of his beloved 354th FG. He stayed with the 354th until the war was over, receiving the PUC. He was discharged Dec. 16, 1945.

He returned to civilian life at the Norfolk Naval Base in Virginia as a firefighter, but often recalled his long days and longer nights watching the P-51 pilots land or attempt to land, hoping he would not have to watch another crash or pull another pilot from a burning plane. He was proud of his service to the brave men of the 9th Air Force and thinks of it often.

Now retired for more than 20 years, he enjoys life on a mountain top in rural Virginia, with his wife of 55 years. His one son is a successful banker in Washington, DC, who is very proud of his father and visits him often.

WILLIAM B. FOSTER, 2nd lieutenant, pilot, born Jan. 7, 1922 at Abbyville, KS. He joined the USAAC at Dallas, TX in November 1942 and was called to active duty in February 1943, Sheppard Field, TX. Primary flight training was at Sikeston, MO, PT-19; basic flight training, Strother Field, KS, BT-13; advance flight training, Aloe Field, Victoria, TX, AT-6; Aerial Gunnery, Matagorda Island, TX, P-40; and Goldsboro and Wilmington, NC, P-47 training.

Joined the 362nd FG as a replacement pilot on Nov. 1, 1944 and was shot down on his 13th mission by enemy ground fire during the Battle of the Bulge on Dec. 23, 1944. Taken prisoner and sent to Stalag Luft I prison camp on the Baltic Sea until freed by Soviet troops April 30, 1945.

Married in April 1947 to Beulah Dunn, they have three daughters, seven grandchildren and 10 great-grandchildren. Retired in 1995 and presently lives in a retirement complex in Hutchinson, KS.

WILLIAM A. FREDRICKS, born Jan. 30, 1925, Grand Island, NE and grew up in Snyder, NE. Entered service on Aug. 14, 1943 and took basic training with Aviation Engineers at March Field, CA.

Left Nov. 20, 1943 for a Repo Depot at Altringham, England. Joined the 86th Depot Repair Sqdn., 91st ADG, Stansted, England. Left for Chartres, France via Omaha Beach D+90. His squadron was responsible for all major repairs for the 98th BW.

Before completely unpacked, their colonel bet another colonel a month's pay that they could be operational on two bases at once. William was sent on advanced cadre to Cambrai, France, slightly behind the fighting. They changed a tire on a B-26, so he won.

In March 1945 they moved to Liege, Belgium and were scheduled for the South Pacific after the ETO victory, but the A-bomb cancelled that. Left for USA on Aug. 29, 1945. Discharged Nov. 17, 1945, SSgt. Fredricks' awards include the ETO Ribbon w/2 stars, Victory Medal and Unit Citation.

He and his wife of 54 years have one son. Williams is a retired general contractor.

ROBERT W. "BOB" GATES, Colonel, USAF (Ret.), born Jan. 23, 1919, Bradley, SD and joined the service in August 1941. Units served with include 54th FS, P-40s, 1942; 77th BS, B-26, 1942, Alaska and Aleutians; 438th TCG, 87th, 98th, 90th Sqdns. and he was squadron commander, 88th TCS, ETO, 1943-46.

Memorable experiences include when the 438th TCG spearheaded Normandy Invasion dropping 1,420 troopers of 502nd PIR of 101st Abn. Div. at 0046 on June 6, 1944, the first in Normandy; being pilot for Bob Hope USO Troop, September 1942, Alaska and Aleutians; being pilot for Bob Hope USO Show, June/July 1945, Britain, France and Germany.

Commander of Project Hiran and placed 12 radar stations of personnel and Jamesway Huts on top of Greenland icecaps resupplying them using JATO and ski-equipped C-47s. He trained Navy pilots in their ski-equipped R4Q's for mission called Deep Freeze in Antarctic in 1955.

He was commander of Project Ice Skate Task Force and built 5,000 foot ice runway, housing and laboratories for 83 scientists on Ice Island T-3, approximately 40 miles from North Pole, for USA participation in International Geophysical Year – 1956. From 1968-72 he was first commander of 1st Special Operations Wing (Air Commandos), Hurlburt Field, FL.

Awards include Legion of Merit, two DFC, eight Air Medals, Croix de Guerre and PUC. After military retirement in November 1972, he became a realtor, broker and owner of a real estate firm, 1972 to present. He is also a former mayor of Fort Walton Beach, FL, 1979-83 and was instrumental in acquiring USAF enlisted men's widow's home called Bob Hope Village, the home of 256 widows.

Bob has five children, eight grandchildren and six great-grandchildren.

LAURENCE C. GAUGHRAN, born August 1921 in Omaha, NE. Enlisted in USAAC in July 1942 and commissioned as pilot from Moore Field, TX in 1943, received RTU training in Tallahassee, FL. He joined the 510th Sqdn., 405th FG in England and flew 100 missions in the P-47 Thunderbolt. Credited with downing three enemy planes with two probable.

Returned to the States and discharged in 1945. He joined the Colorado Air National Guard, was activated and ordered to Korea in 1951 and served in the IG Department. Retired from the Reserves as lieutenant colonel. His decorations include the Air Medal w/18 clusters, DFC and Silver Star.

During civilian career he was involved in electrical product sales and owned and operated a manufacturing sales agency for 15 years in Omaha, NE before retirement in 1989. Married the former Jean Nelson in 1944, and they have three children, five grandchildren and one great-grandchild.

GEORGE "PAUL" GERBRACHT, enlisted in the US Army, Erie, PA in November 1942 and assigned to USAAF at Miami Beach. In January 1943 he attended American School of Aircraft Instruments in Glendale, CA.

Assigned to 458th Service Sqdn., 318th Service Group at Will Rogers Field, OK, March 1943. As sergeant in the 9th AF he was attached to 434th TC at Aldermaston, England, January 1944, that relocated to Mourmelon le Grand, France in March 1945. After V-E Day the disbanded 458th was reassigned to Pacific duty. Low ASR score ordered transfer to 366th FG at Fritzlar, Germany with dual MOS, instrument and airplane mechanic.

Awarded PUC, Theaters of Operation and Army of Occupation. Discharged in March 1946 and employed as draftsman-electronic technician for 15 years. Retired in 1988 after teaching design drafting 20 years at a vo-tech school. Amateur radio W3QPP since 1950.

Married the former Doris Barlow in Tadley, England in December 1945. They have a son and five grandchildren.

OLIVER L. GOODLANDER, born April 8, 1922, Seymour, IN and grew up in Black River, NY. He enlisted in the USAAC Sept. 28, 1942, one year at Clarkson College. Received pilot wings and commission at George Field, Lawrenceville, IL, Feb. 7, 1944.

Assigned to B-26 crew at Shreveport, LA, flying overseas via the Northern Route to Bishops Stortford, England with the 391st BG, 575th BS. Later, moved to Roye/Ami, France.

A mission on Dec. 23 resulted in the loss of 16 planes and crews. Another mission on Dec. 25, a malfunction prevented dropping the bombs on target and upon trying to land with the load, they ran out of runway, demolishing the plane, but no injuries to crew.

Discharged Dec. 25, 1945, having flown 26 missions and awarded the Air Medal w/4 OLCs and Distinguished Unit Medal.

Graduated Clarkson College with BSME and worked for Texaco, Inc., 1949-83, retiring in Texas. Married Betty Fisk of Watertown, NY and they have three sons and eight grandchildren. Retired, he spends time on Lake Ontario, travel and golf.

LEO GREENFIELD, born in Middletown, NY on Dec. 25, 1923. He enlisted in the Aviation Cadet program in 1942 while attending the University of Miami in Coral Gables, FL. He graduated in Class 44-E at Craig Field, AL, commissioned as a second lieutenant. Trained in P-40s and P-47s and was assigned in 1944 to the 48th FG, 493rd FS, 9th AF, at St. Trond, Belgium.

On his 10th mission while dive bombing a railway yard at Euskirken, Germany, his aircraft was badly damaged by 20mm ground fire. He stayed with his burning aircraft, crossed back into friendly territory and bailed out near Maastricht, Holland. After two weeks of hospitalization, he returned to his unit and completed 38 missions at end of war in Europe. Trained for escort in Pacific but returned to US at war's end.

Decorated with Purple Heart, Air Medal w/4 clusters, PUC and Belgian Fourragere.

After honorable discharge in 1946, he returned to the University of Miami, obtained a juris doctor and a business degree, and has practiced law in south Florida since 1948. In 1959, he married Barbara Anne Merritt. They have two married daughters, one grandson (also named Leo) and on May 2, 2002, celebrated their 43rd anniversary.

He's member of P-47 Thunderbolt Pilots' Association; 493rd Fighter Squadron Association/48th Fighter Group; charter member of the 9th AF Association; former member of The Parents Steering Committee, College of William and Mary; 32nd Degree Mason, Hibiscus Lodge; Mahi Shrine; Board of Directors, Navy League of the United States, Fort Lauderdale Council; member, United States Naval Sea Cadets Support Group.

Community Service: Habitat for Humanity of Broward, Inc. volunteer and Broward Outreach Center, Hollywood, FL, volunteer serviceperson as lecturer;

WILLIAM D. GREENFIELD, Major General, a native of Dayton, OH, he received his wings and was commissioned a 2nd lieutenant in May 1940. Early in 1941, Gen. Greenfield and 12 other pilots went on a special mission to learn the latest fighter tactics by flying Spitfires with some of the "hottest" pilots in the British RAF. In April 1942 he  was sent with the 80th Pursuit Sqdn. to fly combat missions in New Guinea. As commander of the 50th FG in 1944, he and his pilots provided fighter cover for the first wave of landing forces on the Normandy beachhead.

Returning briefly to civilian status in 1945, flying for Trans-World Airlines, he accepted a regular commission in 1946 and was assigned to the Operations Division at Army Air Force Headquarters, Washington, DC. He was appointed Chief of the US Air Force Mission to Venezuela, in 1949. Gen. Greenfield held numerous command assignments in the Air Defense Command, and he also was commander of the 316th Air Division (Defense) in Rabat, Morocco. In July 1964 he was named Assistant Deputy Chief of Staff, Operations, Headquarters ADC, becoming the Deputy Chief of Staff, Operations, Headquarters ADC, in January 1965. He assumed command of the 10th AF in July 1967 and retired as a major general on May 1, 1970.

Decorations include the Distinguished Service Medal, DFC, Bronze Star Medal, Air Medal w/7 OLCs, Croix de Guerre w/palm (Belgium), Croix de Guerre w/palm (France), and Air Force Cross (Venezuela). He has flown 112 combat missions, and is a command pilot with more than 6,000 hours.

Gen. Greenfield married the former Nancy Clark Pribe, of Cincinnati, OH on Oct, 21, 1942. They have three children: William D. Jr., Linda and Ann; seven grandchildren: Geoff, Amelia, Ara, Monica, Luke, Kate and Maggie; and four great-grandchildren: Aidan, Emma, Robin and Lauren.

RICHARD D. GROO, born July 29, 1919, was drafted into the USAAC July 29, 1941. Sent to Cochran Field, a Basic Flying School near Macon, GA; eventually became staff sergeant and Chief NCO for Base Operations. In February 1943 volunteered for combat duty and became cadre for the 362nd FG, Westover Field.  Cadre spent a month at AAFSAT in Orlando before returning to Westover.

Became Chief NCO for 379th FS Operations through OTU training with the group at Westover, Bradley, Groton and Mitchell Field before heading for Camp Shanks and a trip to the ETO aboard the *Queen Elizabeth*. Served in the same capacity (379th Operations) through stations in England, France and Germany.

Awarded Bronze Star in December 1944. The 362nd won numerous battle honors, including the PUC, not once, but twice. Discharged in October 1945.

Currently, retired English teacher with wife and four daughters.

KENNETH HARRIS, born June 12, 1924, New York, NY. He entered military service with the U.S. Army on March 25, 1944. Designated for limited duty in the Spring of 1945, he was transferred from the 84th Inf. Div. to the 1184th Military Police Company attached to HQ, 9th Base Air Depot of the 9th AF, stationed in Compiegne, France where he rose to the rank of staff sergeant.

Discharged from the service in June 1946, he spent the next 38 years as a career registered landscape architect. He is now retired and currently resides in Northport, Long Island, NY with Claire, his wife of 53 years.

JOHN K. "JACK" HAVENER, Lieutenant Colonel, USAFR (Ret.), born Sept. 15, 1920 Sterling, IL and drafted into the Army Infantry in October 1942. In mid-December he transferred to Aviation Cadets, graduated with Class 43-I and was commissioned

Oct. 1, 1943 at Ellington Field, TX. Assigned to 344th BG(M) in Lakeland, FL as a copilot on the Martin B-26 Marauder and went overseas with the outfit in January 1944. He was stationed at #169, Stanstead, Essex and A-59 Cormeilles-en-Vexin, France, eventually attaining unlimited first pilot status.

He was credited with 68 combat missions and decorated with DFC, Air Medal w/2 Silver and two Bronze OLCs, Purple Heart, PUC w/OLC, ETO Medal w/5 BSs, American Theater Medal, Outstanding Unit Ribbon, Reserve Medal w/HG, Longevity Ribbon w/ 1 Silver and one Bronze Leaf, Victory Medal w/Overseas Star.

Returned to the States in February 1945 and was assigned as a 3-26 transition instructor at Laughlin Army Air Field, TX until separation from service in December 1945. Served in the Air Force Reserve until retirement in October 1971 as a lieutenant colonel.

Havener served 39-1/2 years with International Harvester Co. as materials control and production specialist, which included five years of overseas service in England, Turkey and Iran, retiring in 1978. Since retiring he has written two books on the Martin B-26 Marauder and Army Air Force Lyrics and published 22 articles on the Marauder in seven different air-oriented magazines. He is currently vice president of the B-26 Marauder Historical Society.

He was married to Mary Alice Janssen from December 1942 until her death in 1971 and to Doris Orr from 1973 to the present. They have two sons, four grandchildren and five great-grandchildren.

LOREN W. HERWAY, Colonel, born Nov. 3, 1919 in Letcher, SD and grew up near Indianola, IA. Training in Arkansas was followed by Kelly, Randolph and Foster Fields in Texas. Transferred to Westover Field, MA for P-47 training. He then joined the 377th FS of the 362nd FG.

During his USAF career, Col. Herway flew 142 combat missions and logged 389 combat hours within the ETO. He was awarded the Silver Star w/OLC, LOM, DFC w/OLC, Air Medal w/26 OLCs and the AF Commendation Medal.

His service included assignments as Chief, F-104 Weapon System Program Office, Directorate of Tactical and Defense Systems, HQ Air Materiel Cmd.; Chief, Materiel Div., USAF F-104 Office, HQ Aeronautical Systems Div., AF Systems Cmd.; Chief, Program Inspection Div., Office of the Inspector General, HQ AF Systems Cmd.; and as Project Officer, Aeronautical Systems Div., Directorate of Production and Programming, Deputy Chief of Staff, Systems and Logistics, HQ USAF.

He terminated his active military career Aug. 1, 1969 as the special assistant to the Director of Production and Programming, Deputy Chief of Staff, Research and Development, HQ USAF.

Col. Herway was killed in an accident on his farm in West Virginia, Oct. 25, 1988. He and his wife Edna had three sons (one deceased) and 10 grandchildren (one deceased).

JOHN L. HILL, born Aug. 5, 1921, Dawson, GA. Enlisted AAF in April 1942 and commissioned at Luke Field, Class 43-E. Assigned to Westover Field for operational training in P-47s and subsequently to 377th FS, 362nd FG, at Bradley Field, CT. The unit became operational Feb. 8, 1944 in the ETO on a mission led by Col.

Francis Gabreski, one of the leading aces of WWII. 362nd FG was reassigned from 8th to 9th AF prior to D-day.

Flew 93 missions and was awarded the Silver Star, two DFCs, 18 Air Medals and Distinguished Unit Citation. Released from active duty in July 1945, he remained active as a reservist.

Graduated from University of Georgia School of Law in August 1947. Married Sue Tyler in March 1946 and subsequently had three children, three grandchildren and two great-grandchildren. Commenced employment with Hartford Insurance Co. in Atlanta, GA in 1947 and retired from that company as vice president in 1983. Retired from USAF as lieutenant colonel in 1981 and has resided in Vero Beach, FL since 1986.

HAROLD NORMAN HOLT, CO, 366th FG, 9th AF, born May 11, 1916, Philadelphia, PA. He earned his BS degree in commerce, Drexel University, in 1939 and entered the service in June 1939.

He started his own carpet business while in college and expanded it after WWII into Cherry Hill, NJ and Quakertown, PA. Flying Cadet, 42-A, graduated Jan. 2, 1942, then operational flying P-39s, P-40s at France Field, Panama. Assigned CO 390th FS, then CO fighter group prior to invasion of Normandy.

On June 9, 1944, Col. Holt led the 366th as lead group of 18th FGs. which bombed and strafed the area at St. Lo before the break through. This is still the largest fighter plane formation ever recorded in history. He commanded the group throughout the European Campaign to cessation of hostilities in Germany. He flew a total of 156 combat missions and 374 combat flying hours, more than any of the 102 commanders.

In the six weeks following the invasion of Normandy, the 366th FG lost 135 pilots and planes, shot down by ground fire. Although 60% of the pilots either walked out or were taken prisoner, the remaining 40% were gone.

Holt's P-47D, the *Magic Carpet,* was given an affectionate nickname, *The Flying Spare Parts Section,* by service group personnel after combat damage repairs and replacements of three right wings, two left wings, two engines, two tail sections, three sets of gun barrels, two sets of landing gear, two canopies, plus an instrument panel and fuselage tank. His aircraft was credited with 175 combat missions without an abort, a tribute to the ground crew: SSgt. Fritz, Sgt. Tingley, Sgt. Shields, and Sgt. Hayward.

Col. Holt was promoted to the rank of colonel on Nov. 16, 1944, two years and 10 months after graduation from flying school. He was credited with 3-1/2 aircraft destroyed in the air and an unnumbered total on the ground. His awards from ETO operations were the Silver Star, DFC, Bronze Star, French Croix de Guerre w/Palm, Belgian Fourragere, and Air Medal w/27 OLCs, representing additional awards of the medal; Command Pilot.

Continuing his service career, Holt earned MBA at Wharton School, University of Pennsylvania; attended Harvard Advanced Management Program; served several years in Pentagon Staff assignments; CO of 81st FW, converting that wing to an atomic capability; commanded Squadron Officer School; Director of Research, Development, Production and Logistics on US NATO Staff; served as U.S. Representative to Armaments Committee, NATO; Black Belt (JUDO).

Col. Holt married college classmate Audrey Fremming in 1945. They had two daughters, Cheryl and Linda.

It was With deep sorrow and great pride that the name of Retired Col. Harold Norman "Norm" Holt was added to the call to High Command Roll. He served his country with honor and invested his productivity to build a better America for all. (1916-2001). *Submitted by his wife, Audrey J. Holt.*

WILLIAM GUSTAV HORLACHER enlisted in pre-flight training, Maxwell Field, AL; primary pilot training, Fletcher Field, MS; basic pilot training, Walnut Ridge, AR; advanced pilot training, Craig Field, AL; and Transition Training, P-47, Westover Field, MA.

His battles and campaigns include Northern France, Air Offensive Europe, Normandy, Rhineland and Ardennes. Received Air Medal w/16 OLCs, DFC, EAME Ribbon w/6 BSS and two Overseas Bars. Served as P-47 Fighter Pilot with 9th AF in England and France for 17 months. Flew 110 missions over Europe and was discharged April 28, 1943.

After discharge, he flew for Storer Broadcasting Co., New York; Mackey Airlines, Florida; and 25 years (1957-81) with Eastern Airlines, Georgia. He built model airplanes as a hobby and took 1st place with his CUB, in Pretty Place Contest, Atlanta R/C Club, April 1984.

Married since 1945, he has four children, six grandchildren and three great-grandchildren. William passed away Feb. 14, 1998.

DONALD B. HYDE, born Jan. 29, 1924 in Pawtucket, RI. While attending Brown University in 1942, he enlisted in the Enlisted Reserve Corps on October 26 and was called to duty Feb. 16, 1943. After being fitted out at Fort Devens, MA, he went to pre-meteorology school at Amherst College, MA where he was washed out after six months. He then went to BTC #10 at Greensboro, NC, and finally to Chanute AFB for the weather observer course.

In order to get to his first permanent assignment he went to Jefferson Barracks, MO, Camp Kilmer, NY, across the ocean on the *Queen Elizabeth,* Dunham Park, Marbury Hall, Hospital 168 at Stockton Heath, Marbury Hall again, Bruche Hall and Billy Mitchell Hall. Three months later he was on the move again, Tinker Hall, Bruche Hall, Tinker Hall and finally to RAF St Mawgan, Newquay, Cornwall. This was one of his longer stays, six months.

On Dec. 24, 1944 he flew to Paris spent Christmas down town and on December 26, flew to Marignane (Marseilles). In February 1945 he saw a notice on the bulletin board which said "Volunteer for the 21st Weather Squadron." He did, and on February 17 flew to Paris and to Dijon the next day, where he was met by troops in a personnel carrier and was driven to Vittel, France by way of the front near Mulhouse. Up until now he had been in the 8th AF, now he was in the 9th.

On April 23 the whole outfit moved to Heidelberg but kept the same designation, Det. KK. Less than two months later the detachment was deactivated and he was transferred at Det. YJ at Echterdingen (Stuttgart).

The war was over and people were anxious to go home but first one had to have enough points. Don had two Battle Stars so that helped a bit. In the meantime the detachment had so many people they only worked 10 days a month so he became a tourist and took leaves in Paris, Nice, a bus trip to Antwerp with stops at Luxembourg and Bruxelles and a trip via personnel carrier to Constance, Innsbruck, northern Italy, Dachau and Munich. On October 23 Det. YJ was deactivated and he moved to Bad Kissingen for two months, then a train ride (40 and 8) to the Calas staging area and boat trip on the SS *Mormacport* from Marseilles to Hampton Roads and a bus trip to Fort Patrick Henry arriving there at 2300 Dec. 24, 1945.

On December 29 he was back where it all began, Fort Devens, MA. He was discharged on Jan. 1, 1946 after enlisting in the reserves. He went back to Brown again and graduated in 1949. After looking around for a job he enlisted again as a PFC on Oct. 6. He was never in the 9th again, had four tours in England and one in Spain. He was stationed at Goodfellow AFB, Scott AFB, Cheyenne Mountain and Sunnyvale in the States.

He married Isabel Bourgeois on Jan. 27, 1951 and had four children. Bel died Nov. 21, 1968 at the Presidio of San Francisco. He went back to England and in early 1970 the husband of his second cousin died. After waiting what he considered a decent time, he proposed by mail and she went over to England to be married. He went to Spain in 1971 and after three years came to Pease AFB where he retired in December 1974. Don never knew what he wanted to be until he retired. He never worked again.

After retirement he lived in Kennebunk, ME with Sally, daughter Martha, and son Don Jr. The other two had gone off, Mary was married and Mark was continuing his college career. Martha and Don ultimately joined the military, she in the AF and he in the Army. Martha retired in 2001 as a SMSgt just like her father. In June 2002 Don Jr. made full colonel. In April 1988 Don Sr. had a stroke, and in June 1992 they made a move to Colorado Springs where there are around 100 retired weathermen. It felt just like home.

MICHAEL N. INGRISANO JR., enlisted Sept. 3, 1942 in New York City. After being assigned to the USAAC, he was sent to Miami for basic training. Then on to Chicago, IL, for training as a radio operator/ mechanic. His first assignment was with the 72nd TCS based in Alliance, NE. In July 1943, he volunteered for overseas duty as a member of a replacement crew.

On August 17, he joined the 37th TCS, 316th TCG in El Kabrit, Egypt. After flying supply missions in support of the British Army and RAF, the squadron joined the rest of the 316th in Sicily. In February 1944, the Group was sent to England, and continued training for the invasion of France. He participated in the Normandy invasion, four missions in the invasion of Holland, and his final combat mission was the paradrop of the British airborne into Wesel, Germany (Operation Varsity).

During his 21 months overseas, he flew 1,500 hours, was awarded three Air Medals, the Distinguished Unit Citation W/2 OLCS, and nine Battle Stars. He was honorably discharged on Sept. 3, 1945.

After WWII, he attended Rockhurst University in Kansas City, MO where he received a BS in Literature in 1948, and by 1949, received a MA in literature from the State University of Iowa.

From 1949-52, while serving as an instructor in the English department, he also concentrated on his literature and history studies. He then worked in public affairs in the electronics industry, and with the US Customs Service until he retired in 1988. He wrote numerous historic articles for the Customs Service, and still writes book reviews for a Civil War publication. He is the author of *An Artilleryman Man's War. Gus Dey and the 2nd United States Artillery,* (published in 1998); *Valor Without Arms: A history of the 316th Troop Carrier Group, 1942-1945* (2001); and *And NothingIs Said: Wartime Letters,* August 5, 1943-April 21, 1945. (2002). He continues to publish articles on WWII for the *9th AFA Flyer, the American Airborne Association Quarterly,* and for *BOTNA* (Buddies of the Ninth Association) for whom he was named an honorary president for the year 2003-2004. He also contributed to the 9th AFAs upcoming history.

LEWIS A. JOHNSON, Corporal, born May 23, 1923, Underwood, WA. He enlisted in the USAAC Nov. 25, 1942; took basic training at Fresno, CA, December 1942; Radio School at Chicago, January to May 1943.

Assignments: June-October 1943, Will Rogers Field with 409th BG; October-December 1943, Woodward AB, OK; December 1943-February 1944, DeRidder AB, LA.

Left Camp Shanks, NY on Feb. 27, 1944 and arrived in England March 7, 1944. Served as VHFDF Operator, 409th BG, 642nd BS, A-20 aircraft at Little Walden, England, March to September 1944; Bretigny, France, September 1944-February 1945; Laon, France February-June 1945; Camp New York, France (Reims), June-July 1945.

Returned to the States Aug. 15, 1945 and discharged in September 1945. His awards include the EAME Campaign Medal w/6 Bronze Stars, Good Conduct Medal and American Campaign Medal.

Returned to Seattle and married in 1945. Worked in control tower at Boeing Field, then moved to Portland, OR in 1948 where he was radio and TV repairman until retirement in 1986.

LLOYD L. JOHNSON, born in Oakdale, NE on Oct. 9, 1923. He graduated from Oakdale High School in 1941, enlisted in the USAAC and graduated from Single Engine Fighter School at Luke AFB, Phoenix, AZ on April 16, 1944.

He joined the 50th FG, 81st FS and flew the P-47 "Thunderbolt" with the 9th AF in Europe. He flew 99 combat missions and is credited with two aerial victories, including a ME-262 jet fighter. He joined the Nebraska Air National Guard after the war and retired after 41 years of military service as the ANG Chief of Staff and as a brigadier general.

He is one of the founders of the 9th AF Association, one of the directors and has served as the association president and chairman.

Lloyd and Barbara have three children, 10 grandchildren and three great-grandchildren. They are both retired and enjoy the leisurely life-style of townhouse living. They live in Lincoln, NE.

ROBERT H. JONES, born Nov. 22, 1918, resided in Stratford, NJ and was a member of the United Methodist Church for over 65 years. Bob passed away on June 27, 1996. He joined the Army on April 28, 1941, being assigned to artillery and following the attack on Pearl Harbor, he volunteered to join the USAAC, becoming an officer. When asked why he wanted to fly, since he had never been near an airplane, he asked a pilot, "Do you eat food from a can?" The reply was no, "Do you sleep in foxholes?" The reply was no, "then you can count on me."

He completed his multi-engine training at Williams Air Base in June 1943, and instead of bombers he was assigned to fly P-38 Lightings. They were one of the ultimate fighters during WWII and most pilots only dreamed of flying them. He was sent to China-Burma-India Theater where he flew 52 missions with the 449th FS.

On Nov. 11, 1944, they ran into a group of Zeros where he shot down two. One was a head on at 20,000 feet and the other was when he heard his friend yelling on the radio, "I can't get him off me." They were below him and in a tight turn when he hit the Zero with a defection shot.

He received the Air Medal and in January 1945 he was awarded the DFC, signed by Major General Claire Chennault, of the Flying Tigers. He retired November 1968 as a major in the USAFR.

Married 46 years to Hazel, they had two sons, Robert and Donald, and six grandchildren: Donald, Tracey, Denise, Keith, Danielle and David. He is missed.

JACK J. KELLAR, enlisted in USAAC at Hamilton Field, CA and put in his basic training at "Goon" hill at Hamilton in October 1942. He spent four months at A&E School at Love Field, Dallas, TX, then to Alison Engine School at Indianapolis, IN then another basic training at Hammer Field, CA.

Assigned to the 380th FS of the 363rd FG at Santa Rosa, CA (Kellar's home town) then a trip to England on the *Queen Elizabeth I* to the 9th AF in southern England where they got their P-51 Mustangs. He was crew chief on A9-B and P-51.

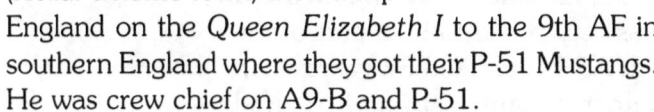

After six months in England they were off to Cherbourg, France, followed by Luxemborg, Belgium, Holland and finally Germany where he was when the war was over.

Jack was married to Alice Streeter before going into the service and they celebrated their 60th wedding anniversary April 5, 2002. They have two daughters and five grandchildren.

He was a co-owner of Santa Rosa Auto Parts and Santa Rosa Bearing Co. from 1951 to retirement in 1972.

ROBERT W. KELLER, completed Civilian Pilot Training Program and received private pilot's license in 1940. Graduated from Franklin & Marshall College in 1941, enlisted at Harrisburg, PA, for Aviation Cadet Program, Class 42F, at Maxwell Field, AL and commissioned in June 1942 at Moody Field, GA.

Assigned to MacDill Field, FL, for B-26 training. Upon completion became B-26 instructor pilot. In April 1943 assigned as Operations Officer of the newly formed 558th BS, 387th BG and flew across Atlantic Ocean in June 1943 to base in England. Became 558th Sqdn. CO in April 1944 and was lead pilot of group maximum effort on D-Day afternoon mission. He flew 62 missions over Europe until V-E Day. Remained in Air Force and retired as colonel in 1971. Awarded the Legion of Merit w/OLC, DFC w/OLC, Air Medal w/10 OLCs, Commendation Medal, Distinguished Unit Medal, French Croix de Guerre, and six Campaign Ribbons.

Married to the former Laurie Brown of East Aurora, NY, in 1943. They have two children and reside in San Rafael, CA.

DR. RICHARD KIK, attended Western Michigan University and graduated with BA degree in pre-med. Entered Cadets in August 1942 and graduated from Luke Field, AZ on May 20, 1943 in Class 43-E.

Assigned to Westover Field to train in P-47s, then to 9th AF in England with 368th BG. Flew out of Chilborten, England until June 1944, then moved to Normandy, Strip A-3. He was stationed at two other bases in France and Belgium. He flew 120 sorties before returning to States in October 1944.

Assigned to training command and instructed advanced flyers at Stewart Field, NY where he taught West Point Cadets. He enrolled in college in 1945 and attended Midwest University College of Osteopathy Medicine. Graduating in 1953 he entered family practice in 1954 until retirement in 2001 in Richmond, MI. He is still active in medicine and deputy medical examiner for Kalamazoo County, MI.

His decorations include the Silver Star, two DFCs, Air Medal w/15 clusters and DUC. He was officially discharged from the USAFR in 1956.

Married Betty Jackson on May 26, 1943 and they celebrated their 60th wedding anniversary in 2003. They have two sons, five grandchildren and two great-grandchildren.

VIRGIL P. KIRKHAM, born Nov. 27, 1924 in Corbett, OR. He enlisted in the US Army at age 18, was inducted in January 1943 and became a first lieutenant. He spent his career in the 362nd FG, 377th FS. He flew P-47s for 82 missions, before he volunteered for the 83rd when he was shot down April 30, 1945, over the forests outside of Ujzed, Czechoslovakia. The town saw   the plane crash and put out the fires, but Virgil was already gone. They were so moved they erected a monument around the remains of his aircraft and buried him. After the Russians took over the area, they dismantled the monument and took the airplane parts. The town put up a marker and they still remember and honor his memory with the school children bringing flowers to his marker on the anniversary of this date. His family loves and remembers him.

ALBERT H. KNICKLEBINE, born Nov. 15, 1919 in Rochester, IN. He enlisted Jan. 5, 1942 and assigned to 387th BG(M), 556th BS. SSgt. Knicklebine was discharged Oct. 5, 1945. His awards include the Good Conduct Medal, ETO Medal w/5 stars, Victory Medal, DUC and French D-Day Medal. He is presently retired.

MAX KUSHNER, Lieutenant Colonel, USAF (Ret.), enlisted in USAC Sept. 6, 1940. Graduated Aircraft Mechanics School, Curtis Wright Aeronautical University, Chicago, IL in July 1941. Transferred to First Air Base Sqdn. at Mitchell Field, NY and became crew chief on various aircraft, namely AT-6, VC-78 and B-23.

In August 1943 he went to England, became master sergeant and commanded Flight No. 4 of the 36th MR&R Sqdn. They landed on Omaha Beach D-Day + 3 on June 9, 1944. By July 1944 he was stationed at Cherbourg in Normandy. He traveled all over France, Belgium, Holland, Luxembourg and Germany, repairing and salvaging all types of aircraft.

Discharged Sept. 30, 1945, activated 1951-53 during Korean War as a 2nd lieutenant and discharged in 1953 as 1st lieutenant. He joined the Air National Guard, commanded 17th CAM Sqdn. at McGuire AFB and discharged as lieutenant colonel in 1977. He received the Meritorious Service Medal.

Graduated Air War College in 1970 and in 1992, at age 70, graduated Broward Community College. Married Jean Israel since 1947. They have three children and two grandchildren. He is currently working for Verizon Wireless Corp.

FORREST R. LAFAYETTE JR., Staff Sergeant, born Oct. 19, 1921, Covina, CA. He joined the service in October 1942 and was assigned to 366th FG. He was crew chief for John Worzer. Forrest was discharged in October 1945.

Forrest had many good memories of his time in the Air Force and was very proud to be a part of the 9th AF. He worked 37 years as an auto mechanic. He and Mildred were married 57 years when he passed away. They had two sons, three grandchildren and 2 great-grandchildren.

WALLACE H. "SAM" LANGELL, Staff Sergeant, born in Lowell, MA and a graduate of Rindge Technical School, Cambridge, MA. His active service was from August 1942 to October 1945. He graduated Radio Operator and Me-

chanics School, Sioux Falls Field, SD, in January 1943. Also completed Tubing and Hydraulics School in Kansas City, MO.

Arrived ETO in 1943, assigned to 434th Group, 73rd TCS, 9th AF as radio operator on C-47 aircraft with 16 combat missions and 636 hours flying time. He acted as navigator and made repairs of equipment in flight.

Decorated with DUC, Air Medal w/2 OLCs, Good Conduct Medal and EAME Campaign Medal w/5 stars. He returned to States in 1945 and was discharged at Sioux Falls AAF.

Employed at Cambridge Electric Light Co. as station electrician for 26 years. He was married 38 years to Agnes McAvoy of Nashua, NH. He passed away in 1983 and is survived by two sons, one daughter, five grandchildren and five great-grandchildren.

NORMAN E. LANGMAID, Lieutenant, born Dec. 7, 1922 in West Warick, RI and graduated from Lockwood High School in June 1940. Norman enlisted in the USAAC in June 1942 and trained at Maxwell Field, Clarksdale, MS and Courtland, AL. He received his wings at Craig Field, Selma, AL, Class of 43-F, completed training at Westover Field, MA and Mitchell Field in Long Island NY and embarked for England Dec. 27, 1943.

Lt. Russell O'Connell, 397th FS, 368th FG, supplied the following information: "Norm, on D-Day was attending a 9th AF school relating to intelligence. I believe that he was the assistant S2 Officer. On June 7th he talked them into giving him an early dismissal so he could go back to the 397th and help. Langmaid was flying the 2nd mission of four that we flew that day and was flying a new airplane that had been assigned to me and I had flown in only a couple of missions when he was shot down. We had not yet transferred the cowling from my old plane with little Oakie on it."

Lt. Langmaid paid the supreme sacrifice on June 7th near Littery France. He was awarded the ETO Medal, American Campaign Medal, Air Medal w/4 OLCs, Purple Heart and had been recommended for the DFC.

JOSEPH L. LAUGHLIN, Colonel, USAF (Ret.), entered flying cadet training at Spartan School of Aeronautics, Tulsa, OK, then Randolph and Kelly Fields, TX. Commissioned in July 1940 and assigned overseas to Wheeler Field, HI, 18th Pursuit Gp., 19th Pursuit Sqdn. and was given command of the 45th FS in January 1943.

Promoted to 1st lieutenant, November 1941; captain, March 1942, major, February 1943. Reassigned Stateside in April 1943; squadron commander, 379th FS, 362nd FG at Westover, MA.

Left for overseas in November 1943 on *Queen Elizabeth* to England, where they set up operations at Wormingford near Colchester, England; April 1944 group moved to Southern England, Headcorn near Maidstone; promoted to lieutenant colonel in March 1944, and became Deputy Group Commander.

In June 1944 the group moved over to France, Station A-12 in Normandy and assigned to XIXth Tactical Command, 9th AF supporting the 3rd Army. Moved to Renne Airport, St. Jaques' Airport, Reims, then Etain, France where they spent the winter of 1944-45. Then to Frankfort Rhein Main, Furth Neurnberg, Illsheim, and after V-E Day moved to Straubing Bavaria, an occupation base.

Assumed command of 362nd Gp. in August 1944 and promoted to colonel in November 1944; Air Command and Staff School, 1947-48; 10th AF HQ Selfridge AFB, MI 1948-51, Director ROTC, Director ANG, Director Operations and Training; Air War College 1951-52; HQ USAF Director Air Defense Division, Director of Requirements, Deputy Chief of Staff R&D, 1952-55; Chief Air Force Section MAAG, Taiwan 1955-57; Wing Commander, 506th Tactical Ftr. Wing, Tinker AFB 1957-59; Commander, 4520 Combat Crew Training Wing, Nellis AFB, 1959-60; Chief of Staff 12th AF, Waco, TX, 1960-61; TAC HQ Director of Training, 1961-63, Langley AFB; Deputy Chief of Staff Operations, 17th AF, Ramstein, Germany, 1963-64; Chief of Staff, 17th AF, Ramstein, Germany, 1964-66; Deputy Commander Air Forces Korea, 314th Air Division Osan AFB, 1966-67; Senior Air Force Advisor US Army Field Artillery Center, Ft. Sill, OK 1967-69.

Retired after 30 years in November 1969. His decorations include Silver Star, LOM, DFC w/OLC, Air Medal w/15 OLCs, American Defense Service Medal w/Bronze Star, American Campaign Medal, Asiatic/Pacific Campaign Medal w/Bronze Star, EAME Campaign Medal w/7 Bronze Stars, WWII Victory Medal, Army of Occupation Medal, PUC w/OLC, AF

Longevity Service Award + clusters for 30 years and French Croix De Guerre w/Palm.

Joseph and Audrey Jean married in October 1945; they have four children and four grandchildren.

JAMES THOMAS LEE, Sergeant, born April 6, 1924, New York City, NY. Attended Radio School, Class 9, Scott Field, IL and was radio operator, AAF 765, 67th TRG, 30th PRS Sqdn.

Memorable experience was driving a 6x6 and towing a generator across the Rhine River on a Pontoon Bridge at Remagan – the first time he had ever driven a vehicle.

Discharged Sept. 22, 1945, his awards include the American Campaign, EAME Campaign, Good Conduct, WWII Victory Medal, Marksman Carbine and six Battle Stars.

James and his wife Adrianna have two children, James and Jane. His civilian occupation was photography and he had a studio in Easton, MD. Now retired his hobby is wood carving, building model boats currently building an aircraft carrier.

JACK A. LEMOS, joined the USAAC on Aug. 4, 1942. Graduated from Radio Operator School at Truax Field, Madison, WI. Graduated Control Tower Operator School at Chanute Field, IL, became an instructor there and later assigned to Control Tower Operator at Robbin's Field, GA.

Sent to England in 1943 and assigned to the 9th AF and trained for overseas combat at Middle Wallop. He was involved in D-Day invasion at Normandy.

Earned campaign medals for EAME sector, Rhineland-Central European sector and was decorated with the "Battle of the Bulge" and Belgian Fourragere for meritorious service during Battle of Ardennes. He was discharged in October 1945.

Resides in his birthplace, Mendocino, CA, and retired after 37 years with local utility company. He also served 62 years with Volunteer Fire Department. Married in 1948 to the former Antoinette Robinson of Los Angeles. He is the father of seven children and has 14 grandchildren and seven great-grandchildren.

AUGUSTINE PATTERSON LITTLE JR., Colonel, born Nov, 17, 1914, Louisville, GA. Graduated West Point in 1937, eighth in his class, and married Martha Helen Fielis the day after graduation. They had two children, Augustine Patterson Little III and Barbara Lee Little.

Stationed with Corps of Engineers at Fort Benning, GA, he earned master's of civil engineering from MIT in 1940. Served at Langley Field and Fort Belvoir, VA; executive officer of 813th Engineer Aviation Battalion (EAB), McChord Field, WA; joined 8th AF in Savannah, GA; commanded 814th EAB during invasions of both northern Africa and Italy. The 814th EAB was only aviation engineer battalion in forward area and was in forefront of African Campaign.

Took command of 922nd Engr. Avn. Regt. in Spring 1944, landed on Omaha Beach at H+8 hours, "Point Regiment" for IX Engr. Cmd. Promoted to colonel July 22, 1944. He was mortally wounded during reconnaissance mission of Le Bourget Airfield outside Paris, Aug. 27, 1944 while rescuing his wounded driver. He died of wounds two days later and was buried in Normandy-American Cemetery, Colleville-sur-Mer.

Awarded Legion of Merit, Soldier's Medal and posthumously awarded Croix de Guerre avec Palme, Silver Star and Purple Heart.

RAYMOND P. LOWMAN, Colonel, USAF (Ret.), born May 14, 1921 at Geary, OK. Entered Aviation Cadet Training in 1942 and graduated in Class 43-B from Foster Field, TX.

Deployed to England with the 365th FS, 358th FG in September 1943 and flew 78 combat missions in the P-47, including 41 as flight commander. He spent 10 months as a German POW.

Remained in service after WWII and initially assigned to AMC and AACS, then to Strategic Air Command in 1950. He held many responsible positions including B-29, B-47 Aircraft Commander, Wing Chief Standardization, Squadron Commander, Wing Director Operations, Division DO, Chief Eighth Air Force Command Center, Vice Commander of 99th and 100th BWs, and Commander of the 17th and 70th BWs. He flew combat missions in Vietnam while Commander of the 70th and has over 7,000 pilot flying hours and holds numerous awards and decorations including the Legion of Merit.

Established and served as president of his own printing firm from 1973 until sold in 1991. Served as director, vice president, president and chairman, Board of Directors of the 9th AF Association.

Married in 1945 to Olga Lewis and has three sons: Col. Raymond P. Lowman II, USA (Ret); Dr. Rodney L. Lowman and Dr. Kenneth K. Lowman.

EDWARD F. MACLEAN died at age 77 on Jan. 10, 1999. Foe of Hitler, friend of education, family man, co-founder and first president of the 9th Air Force Association.

A WWII veteran P-47 fighter pilot who flew a remarkable 97 missions against Nazi, Germany in just one year

and served 25 years on three different school boards of education in his hometown of Valley Stream, NY.

A lifelong resident of Valley Stream, Ed was first sent to Europe (England, Colchester) in April 1943 aboard the *Queen Elizabeth* after training at Bradley, Westover and Mitchell Fields.

Like his record of all activities, it was sharp and dynamic - 97 missions in 12 months. He won the DFC and 26 Air Medals. With the rank of first lieutenant he was discharged in October 1944, being saved from the Far East by Harry's Bomb at Hiroshima. Ed enjoyed 55 years of wedded bliss and did everything right. He is survived by two sons, two daughters, his wife and seven grandchildren.

MORTON D. MAGOFFIN, Colonel, USAF (Ret.), growing up in a small town in Minnesota, he never dreamed that one day he would be a graduate of West Point, go on to flying school, be at Wheeler Field in Hawaii on Dec. 7, 1941 and go on to be an ACE fighter pilot and holder of the DSC.

He was invited to be observer on the *Hornet* when Doolittle raiders

hit Japan, April 18, 1942. Mort was group commander of the 362nd FG (known as Mogin's Maulers) and flew 85 missions before he was shot down Aug. 10, 1944 over France and captured. He was fortunate that the Americans liberated Paris shortly thereafter and he was hidden in an armoire by a young French girl to avoid being taken by the Germans.

After spending some time in a French hospital, where he underwent immediate surgery on his right leg, he was sent to England for more medical treatment. After recovery, he served in California and Alaska, then to the Air War College in Montgomery, AL, thence to the Pentagon in War Plans for two years. Mort was then sent to Korea to be in charge of the air base in Seoul for one year.

Mort retired with medical disabilities on March 19, 1958. His wife of 34 years died in 1973, and he remarried in 1975 and still lives in Pleasanton, CA with his second wife of 27 years.

Due to major surgery and a stroke in 2000, Mort is confined to the house with full-time care, but he is very fortunate to be able to speak, walk and do limited things, but no longer able to travel. He misses his old military friends and the reunions, but has many fond memories.

CHARLES F. "CHUCK" MANN, born Aug. 14, 1924 McKenzie, TN, attended Bethel College and University of Tennessee, then enlisted in USAAC Aviation Cadets, San Antonio Aviation Cadet Center; PT-19 Primary, Pine Bluff, AR; BT-14 basic, Independence, KS; AT-6 advanced, Moore Field Mission, TX with commissioning Class 44-C. Following P-47 Fighter Schools at

Richmond, VA, Goldsboro and Wilmington, NC, Chuck was assigned to 377th FS of 362nd FG "the Maulers," XIX TAC, 9th AF, in Rheims, France, October 1944.

Rocket and dive-bombing missions in close support of Gen. Patton's Third Army during Battle of the

Bulge and Crossing of the Rhine were his proudest fare. He destroyed ME-109 over the Remagen Bridge, then shot down a long-nosed FW-190, three days later, after receiving an ankle wound from ground fire.

Recipient of the Silver Star, 13 Air Medals, Purple Heart and two DUCs. After V-J Day the group returned to Seymour-Johnson Field, Goldsboro, NC. Chuck reverted to civilian life and reserve status while graduating from Murray State (KY) in physics and chemistry.

Continuing fighter flying in the USAFR and TNANG, he was recalled to active duty 1951-53 during the Korean War. He retired from the Tennessee Air Guard in 1965 after various Flying, Operations, Intelligence and Personnel assignments in Wing Headquarters.

Chuck's civilian careers included 22 years with Crane Co. in sales and management, followed by establishment of a manufacturers agency partnership with his wife, Fern. He was an International Aerobatic Club competitor, judge and committee chairman, and built an aerobatic airplane.

In 1959 Chuck co-founded the 362nd FG Assn. and was secretary for 10 years. He was a founder of the 9th AF Assn., serving as director, secretary and vice-president, administration until his death in 1998.

DANIEL F. MCALLASTER, enlisted in USAAC in October 1942; graduated Air Mechanics School, Keesler Field and Hydraulics School, Chanute Field in 1943. Assigned to 30th Photo Reconnaissance Squadron, Will Rogers Field in October 1943.

Arrived Chalgrove, England in February 1944. Many hours were spent getting the squadron operational. The main thrust was mapping all of Europe prior to D-Day, especially the coastal areas. Moved to France last of June

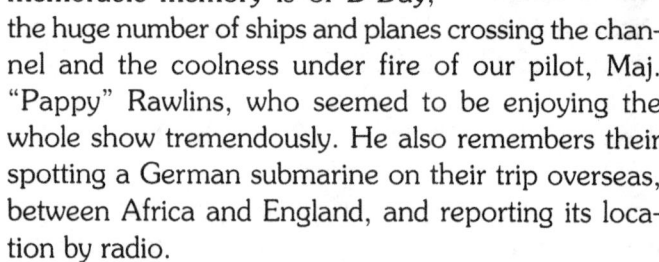

1944 then to Belgium and Germany. The 30th Photo Reconnaissance Squadron was the first squadron in the 9th AF and the first squadron to operate from Normandy and Germany. The 30th received the DUC in January 1945.

Sgt. McAllaster was discharged in October 1945 and went into flour milling. Retired in 1987 after 41 years of being in the wheat industry. Married Faye Johnson in 1943, has two children, three grandchildren and one great-grandchild.

JOHN O.C. MCCRILLIS, Tech Sergeant, born June 3, 1914 in Brocton, MA. Enlisted May 18, 1942 and served with 488th Med. BS as radioman/gunner on a B-25. Flew 50 missions over north Africa, Sicily and southern Italy.

Discharged Sept. 18, 1945. He received the Air Medal w/9 OLCs.

After discharge he graduated Rhode Island School of Design, 1939, with a BFA in 1950 and MFA from Yale University in 1952. He taught calligraphy for 50 years and is still active as a calligrapher and graphic designer. He's retired from Yale University Press where he served for 27 years.

GEORGE V. MCDEVITT, joined the USAAC in August 1942. Graduated from Chicago Radio School in December and assigned to 77th TCS, 435th TCG at Pope Field, NC. He flew to England in October 1943 and stayed with the 77th until his discharge in August 1945.

Participated in glider drop on D-Day, Invasion of Southern France, Invasion of Holland, supply missions at Bastogne for the "Battered Bastards" and numerous supply and medical evacuee missions. Most memorable memory is of D-Day,

the huge number of ships and planes crossing the channel and the coolness under fire of our pilot, Maj. "Pappy" Rawlins, who seemed to be enjoying the whole show tremendously. He also remembers their spotting a German submarine on their trip overseas, between Africa and England, and reporting its location by radio.

George was awarded the Air Medal w/4 OLCs, ETO Ribbon w/7 Battle Stars and the PUC. He attained the rank of staff sergeant. He lives with his wife Mary Jane, a former Woman Marine corporal, in Vero Beach, FL.

WILLIAM E. MCKAIN, enlisted in the USAAC Aug. 24, 1942 and was called to active duty Jan. 23, 1943. Pilot training was at Texas A&M, Vernon, TX;

Garden City, KS; graduated Aloe Field, Victoria, TX; and started P-47 training, Goldsboro, NC and Wilmington, NC.

Sent to England to escort bombers with 8th AF, then in November was sent to Etain Field, France to 362nd FG. Put in 60 missions on March 25, 1945, went through bomb blast, landed plane, flipped over on him, back broken, first lumbar section crushed.

He was hospitalized until his discharge Sept. 6, 1946. Awards include the Air Medal w/Silver Star, four Bronze OLCs, DUB, Purple Heart, American Theater Ribbon w/2 Bronze Battle Stars and six Overseas Victory Medals.

He taught school until retirement in 1980. William married Dorothy Lyons in June 1941 before he enlisted. They have three children, five grandsons and one great-granddaughter.

JOHN K. MCMAHON, inducted into USAAC in February 1943; trained in Santa Ana, Tulare and Lemoore, CA. Commissioned Luke Field in Phoenix, March 1944, Class 44-C, then assigned to Harding Field, Baton Rouge, LA for P-47 training.

Transferred to Pilot Replacement Depot, Shrewsbury, England, July 1944; attached to 9th AF, 362nd FG, 379th FS, August 1944. Flew combat missions in Rennes, Reims and Etain, France to strafe enemy ships (Brest Harbor) and automated cavalry.

Promoted to 1st lieutenant, December 1944, he was downed and killed by gunfire over Luxembourg, Jan. 22, 1945 on his 48th mission. Decorated posthumously with Presidential Citation, DFC, Purple Heart, one Silver and one Bronze OLCs added to Air Medal.

McMahon graduated Fort Dodge Community College and attended Regis College in Denver. Originally buried in Hamm American Military Cemetery in Luxembourg, his remains were transferred to Corpus Christi Cemetery, Fort Dodge, IA. *Submitted by Bonnie K. McMahon, widow of Jack's brother, Donald V. McMahon, honorary member of 362nd FG Assn.*

KENNETH F. "KEN" MCNEELY, enlisted in the USAF in 1950 and graduated from AF Clerk Typist Course, University of Alabama. First duty station was San Marcos AFB, TX. This was the start of a career as an agent of the US Government in the acquisition area.

Served as Cash Purchasing Officer and Class "C" Agent, Finance Officer in Korea 1956-57. From 1957-60 he was assigned to HQ 9th AF Force, Shaw AFB, SC in the Directorate of Procurement. As this directorate phased out, he served as the director from April through June 1960. Transferred to the Directorate of Procurement, HQ Tactical Air Command, Langley AFB, VA to perform MAJCOM staff surveillance of all TAC Base Procurement Offices.

He also served as contracting officer to obtain billeting for recalled reservist during the Cuban crisis. Taught Government Contracting courses at Amarillo AFB, November 1962-May 1966. Served as contracting officer for Air Force and Navy research in the European Office of Aerospace Research, 1966-70; technical advisor for contracted operations in Laos, 1972-73, while assigned to DEPCHJUSMAG, Udorn, Thailand; served as civilian contracting officer at Sheppard AFB, TX, the Aerospace Guidance and Metrology Center, Newark AFS, OH; and Dyess AFB, TX. Retired from the Air Force in 1996.

Married to the former Ramona Klemann since April 11, 1952. They have four children, eight grandchildren, and two great-grandsons.

RAMONA MCNEELY, entered Civil Service as a secretary in Tac Ops, 9th AF in the summer of 1958. She was a young mother and wife of TSgt. Ken McNeely. In the summer of 1959 she was promoted to a secretary in the 9th AF Personnel Office.

Following her husband she continued secretarial work at HQ TAC,

Amarillo AFB, and with the Foreign Agricultural Service in Brussels, Belgium.

Stateside saw her with OTS at Lackland, OSI at Dyess, and finally, after completing her education, she entered instructor duty at Sheppard AFB, TX. Before retiring from the Faculty Development Branch in November 1990, Ramona had earned a master's of education degree and the Air Force Master Instructor rating. Now she and her husband, a retired senior master sergeant and GS-11, enjoy their grandchildren, volunteer work and travel.

HARMON T. MERWIN, born July 10, 1920 in Middlefield, OH and attended Kent State University. Worked at Goodyear Aircraft in Akron, OH as a sheetmetal worker. Enlisted in the USAAC Oct. 12, 1942 and assigned to the 76th Air Service Squadron.

Landed in England June 1, 1943 and stationed at Colchester, Chelmsford and Great Dunmo. He was in London when the first V-1 bomb landed. V-1s flew over base and a piloted aircraft bombed the base resulting in two deaths and numerous injuries.

Stationed in France, Belgium and in Germany for six months in the Army of Occupation. Served on a mobile unit which serviced aircraft for the 386th BG. The service included repair of damage and replacement of parts as necessary on the bases and in the field. He was discharged Jan. 1, 1946 as a sergeant.

Graduated from Ohio State University as a landscape architect and worked as a regional planner and director of the Franklin and Mid-Ohio Regional Planning Commissions in Columbus, OH. Retired Jan. 1, 1986. A member of American Society of Certified Planners, president, Ohio Chapter and president of the Ohio Planning Conference. Received numerous awards in planning and is listed in Marquis *Who's Who's in the Midwest.*

Married to the former Eldred Stahman since 1954, they have two living and one deceased child. One child is a career medic in the US Army.

ARTHUR R. MILOW, Major, completed flight training at Muskogee, OK, Brady, TX and Kelly Field, TX. Commissioned 2nd lieutenant, USAAC in Class of 1941-I. Flew desert maneuvers out of Blythe, CA in 1942, transferred to Will Rogers Field, OK, in 1943 to 409th BG.

Milow was commander of 643rd Sqdn. for 26 months. He flew A-20 and A-26 aircraft for a total of 66 combat missions in the ETO. Separated from the Army in May 1946 and recalled in 1962 to Active Duty at Homestead AFB for the Cuban Missile Crisis as a lieutenant colonel Ops Staff Officer. Decorations include the DFC, Air Medal w/12 OLCs and EAME w/6 Battle Stars.

Retired in 1978 after 32 years with Pan American World Airways as B-747 Captain. Hobby is "running" and still participates in 5K's, 10K's, and 1/2 marathons. Milow was Class of 1940 at University of Nebraska, Omaha. Married to Bette Urquhart for 60 years, with five daughters, six granddaughters and two great-grandchildren.

PAUL D. MITCHELL, born Aug. 27, 1915 in Atlanta, GA. Entered active service Aug. 17, 1942 and assigned to HQ, Miami Beach, FL until Oct. 28, 1943 as assistant post intelligence officer. He served overseas in the ETO for 21 months; assigned to HQ 362nd FG from Feb. 8, 1944 to Aug. 2, 1945 as the public relations officer.

Returned to the US and was assigned to the 301st AAF Base Unit, Drew Field, FL, Aug. 24, 1945 to Feb. 25, 1946 as the public relations officer. He was last assigned to the 326th AAF Base Unit, MacDill Field, Feb. 28, 1946 to July 18, 1946 as the assistant public relations officer. Discharged Nov. 17, 1946.

A 1938 graduate of the University of Florida, where he earned a BA in journalism, he served as editor of *The Record* in the mid-1970s. Prior to that he was a staff writer for the *Florida Times-Union,* worked as a reporter for the *St. Petersburg Times, Lakeland Ledger* and the *Sugar Cane Press,* Clewiston.

Paul and Thelma married in 1942. He passed away Dec. 6, 1997. He was preceded in death by two sons,

Bruce Dayton and Walter Earl. Survivors include his wife Thelma; one daughter, Nona Lee Mitchell Asconi; six grandchildren and two great-grandchildren.

RAYMOND W. MORRIS, First Lieutenant, born Feb. 27, 1922 in Champaign, IL. Enlisted in USAAC in August 1942 and called to active duty as an Aviation Cadet in February 1943. Sent to a College Training Detachment at the University of Montana; Ground School in Santa Ana, CA; primary training in Phoenix, AZ; basic training in Pecos, TX; advanced training, then commissioned at Luke Field in Phoenix, AZ on April 15, 1944.

After P-47 training at Bruning, NE, he was sent to England for some lectures and orientation work. He joined the 362nd Gp., 379th Sqdn. in France and flew 85 missions. Returned home after the war was over and was discharged in October 1945.

Morris is a graduate of San Jose State University having earned a BS in electrical engineering. He was employed at NASA Ames Research Center, Moffett Field, CA for 35 years. Retired in December 1981.

Married since August 1949 to the former Iva Stephens, and they have four children and six grandchildren.

FRANK "PETE" NEASON, enlisted in August 1940 at Chanute Field, IL for Mechanic and Instrument School. In July 1942 he was assigned to the 77th FS, 20th FG in Sarasota, FL, crewing P-39s.

The following October he transferred to the new 8th FW at Dow Field, FL. Their squadron commander suggested they pack sun tans in "B" bag for cold climate.

In November 1942 they sailed on the *West Point*, stopping in Rio De Janerio for fuel, and 17 days later they were in Bomb Bay, India, where they boarded a British ship sailing to Suez. They pitched their tents in the desert near Alamein area on Dec. 22, 1942. They were detailed to work with service squadron behind them and the 79th FG was near.

Moved to Elkabrit in February 1943, then to 26th Air Depot at Devorsor, followed in September 1943 as twin engine cargo flight engineer, Tehran Iran.

JAMES R. NERAL, Lieutenant Colonel (Ret.), born in Johnstown, PA, graduated from high school in 1941 and started college at Penn State College, then was recruited and enlisted in the USAAC in September 1942. He went through the SEAFTC, graduated December 5 as a second lieutenant, assigned to the ATC.

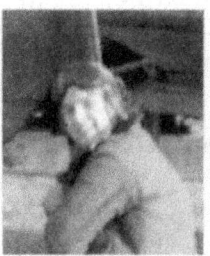 

Re-assigned to B-26s at Barksdale Field and from there to the 394h BG and flew overseas through Greenland and Iceland to England, where he was assigned to the 585th BS.

He flew 49 missions over Europe and was awarded the Air Medal w/8 OLCs, five Battle Stars, EAME Ribbon and the American Defense Ribbon. His Unit was presented with the Croix De Guerre. He remained in the USAFR for 27 years.

James currently resides in Damascus, PA.

DUANE E. OYSTER, born Sept. 24, 1924 in Alliance, OH. He enlisted in USAAC in December 1942 while a student at Ohio State University, at Columbus, OH and called to active duty in March 1943. Entered Aviation Cadets August 1943 with Class 44-A, commissioned Jan. 7, 1944 at Eagle Pass, TX as second lieutenant, AC and assigned to Abilene, TX, Air Base for P-47 training.

Transferred to the 362nd FG, 377th Sqdn. of the 9th AF in Stone, England. Group transferred to Normandy, Rennes, Reims then to Station A-82 Rouvres, France, Nov. 8, 1944. Advanced to first lieutenant, AC, October 1944.

Downed during Battle of Bulge on Jan. 2, 1944 on his 78th mission and was found by 101st Abn. at

Bavigne, Luxembourg and taken to Esch Field Hospital, then returned to his squadron and sent to Medical Review Board in Paris.

Sent home for being unconscious for 16 hours. Decorated with DFC, Purple Heart, four Bronze Campaign Stars, 12 OLCs on Air Medal and Distinguished Unit Citation. Honorably discharged in July 1945.

Oyster is a graduate of Ohio State University, June 1949, earning a BS in mechanical engineering. Married Patricia Fenner in February 1944 in Abilene, TX. They have five children, 11 grandchildren and two great-grandchildren. He is now retired.

THOMAS D. PANTOLIANO, First Lieutenant, enlisted in the USAAC Sept 26, 1942 in Jackson, MS. He had many missions and on his last mission they were flying in formation and an updraft caught his buddy and lifted him up into the undercarriage of his plane. The propeller sliced through the canopy of his buddy and he was killed. Tom's propeller was severely damaged, and he  glided to a landing area. He was a little bruised and shaken up, but was very lucky to walk away from this.

Tom returned to the States and received his honorable discharge on March 11, 1944.

He married Mable Harmon in 1953 and they had six children and seven grandchildren. Tom passed away Nov. 13, 1993.

GEORGE W. PARKER, born May 16, 1923, Joplin, MO. After graduating high school he enlisted July 8, 1940 and went to Airplane Mech School, Chanute Field (December 1940-June 1941). Completed Flying School at Lubbock, TX in Class 42-J; Martin B-26 Transition, Del Rio, TX (January-February 1943).

Assignments: First Minimum Altitude Bomber-Torpedo Unit (B-26 Sqdn.), Eglin Field, flight commander and aircraft maintenance 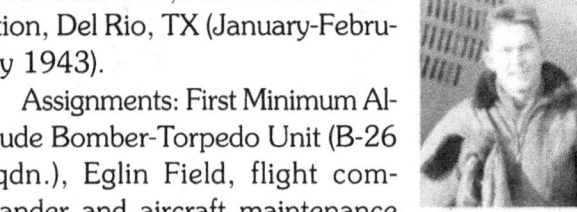 officer; combat tour with 397th BG(M), 596th Sqdn. in ETO, (February 1944- February 1945); flight commander, lead crew, instructor pilot), TDY US Army 19th Corps HQ, G-3 (February -April 1945) as bomb line coordinator. Awards include the DFC, Air Medal w/2 OLCs and Purple Heart w/OLC.

Returned to New York City via the *Queen Mary,* Aug. 2, 1945. Assigned to the US Military Advisory Mission to China, 1946-49; Aircraft Controllers School, Tyndall AFB, AF Intelligence (Pentagon) and Air Force representative. to the Joint Intelligence Objective Agency (1950-54); All-Weather Fighter-Interceptor School, Moody AFB, GA, 1954; Ops officer, 337th FIS Sqdn. (F-89D acft.) Mpls., MN, 1954-55; and 433rd FIS Sqdn., Ladd AFB, AK, Ops Officer; squadron commander 1955-58; assoc. professor and Commandant of Cadets, USAF ROTC, U of Missouri; taught courses in leadership development a world political geography (1958-61).

Earned BS degree at Maryland University, master's degree, Webster University, St. Louis, MO; former Asst. Dean of Extension, Columbia College, MO; Missouri State Representative 1967-73, author of *How To Win An Impossible Election,* insurance sales, real estate broker, founder and past president, B-26 Marauder Historical Society and the National Federation of Pachyderm Clubs. Member Missouri Advisory Committee to the US Civil Rights Commission 1999-present.

Married to the former Lois Oberpriller of Houston, TX, they have four children and eight grandchildren.

WILLIAM A. PARSONS enlisted in the USAAC in 1942 while a student at the University of Kentucky. He was activated in February 1943 and trained in the Southeast Training Command from then until graduation with the Class of 44-E at Spence Field Moultri, GA.

After transition and gunnery at Eglin AFB, he was assigned to   P-47 training at Goldsboro, NC, followed by gunnery and advanced training for combat in Wilmington, NC.

He was assigned to the 377th Sqdn. of the 362nd Gp., 9th AF in January 1945. He was decorated with Air Medal, DFC and Unit Citation. After demobilization Parsons attended the University of Kentucky and Vanderbilt University with a degree of doctor of law.

Retired in 1984, he now fishes and builds birdhouses. He has four children, five stepchildren and 13 grandchildren.

HAROLD PASKOWITZ, born Oct. 13, 1923. He earned an associate degree in business administration from University of Hartford and worked 38 years at Russak Bros. Sand and Gravel Co. as bookkeeper-accountant.

Active duty began Jan. 6, 1943 at Camp Devens with basic training at Sheppard Field, TX. Sent to Arkansas State College for eight weeks training in military administration, then to 442nd FS, Westover Field, MA, to 362nd FG, 379th FS in May 1943, corporal, Intelligence NCO.

Overseas to England in November 1943 to Wormingford Essex and Headcorn Kent; July 1944, Balleroi, A-12 Normandy, France. Their unit moved to various air strips to support Gen. Patton's Third Army.

Memorable experiences include being strafed and shelled by aircraft at Strip A-12, one of their GI's was killed and four wounded in three days.

His awards include the Good Conduct Medal, ETO Ribbon w/6 Campaign Stars and DUB w/OLC.

Harold married Lillian Bromberg on Jan. 2, 1943. They have three sons and one granddaughter.

VITO S. PEDONE, Colonel, USAF (Ret.), born June 30, 1921 in Mount Vernon, NY. Commissioned as a pilot in the USAAC, April 1942. Was assigned to the 8th AF European Theatre as an A-20 light bomber pilot in August 1942. After completing 25 missions, he was assigned to the 9th TC Cmd. HQ as an operation officer. In

January 1943 he was in the initial cadre to form the 9th TC Cmd. Pathfinder Group for the invasion of Normandy. Six IX TC Cmd. Pathfinder, serial of three C-47 aircraft were directed to six drop and landing zones behind Omaha Beach, dropping Pathfinder elements of the 82nd/101st in the evening of June 5, 1944, one-half hour before the arrival of the main air armada and three hours before the beach landings. Col. Pedone was the copilot in the first serial of C-47s and in the first aircraft.

In April 1945, he was assigned to the Command and Staff School at Fort Leavenworth, KS. From 1946-50 he was executive officer to the Task Force Commanders of the Atom Bomb Test Command in the South Pacific for operations: Crossroads-Sandstone and Green House. In January 1951 he was assigned duty with the NATO Air Force Command in Florence, Italy. Upon returning to the US in July, he was assigned to the NATO Military Committee in Washington, DC. In 1959 he was selected to the National War College and graduated in June 1960.

Due to the concern of the Joint Chiefs of Staff that there was no cohesive airlift/airborne planning between the Troop Carrier units of USAF Tactical Air Command and the 82nd and 101st Abn. units of Continental Army Command, a special Joint Airlift Command (consisting of senior officers of TAC 18th AB Corps, 82nd and 101st ABD Military Airlift Command, Air National Guard, and Air Reserves), was activated at Fort Bragg, NC in June 1960. Col. Pedone was assigned as its first commander. This unit was responsible for the combat airlift planning for Cuba in 1961 from home bases to employment bases in southern Florida to the drop zones in Cuba and for turn around operations. The unit received a Presidential Citation for the planning of the three airborne and assault divisions. This would have been the largest airborne operation in US Forces' history.

In September 1962, he became commander of the Department of Defense, Research and Development Field Unit in South Vietnam. Additionally, he was placed on duty with the USAF 1st Air Commando Unit in Bien, Hoa, Vietnam (Farmgate Operation) as a combat pilot. Flew 135 combat missions in the A-26 and C-47 aircraft in support of US Army Special Forces Units. In September 1964 he was assigned to Japan as Director of Operations for the 5th Air Force and to the 41st Air Division as a combat pilot (F-105 aircraft). Participated in combat operation in South East Asia.

Upon returning to the US in 1967, he was appointed Chairman of the Command and Control Committee in the Joint Chiefs of Staff with primary responsibility for briefing senior officials in the Department of Defense and the Executive Branch. Retired as colonel in 1973 after 35 years of duty with the USAF and the NYNG.

Attended North Carolina State College, University of Maryland, BS degree; George Washington University, MS degree; and National War College, Fort Leslie McNair, Washington, DC, Class of 1960.

Participated in combat operations in European Theater (air campaign over Europe and England, Normandy Invasion of France, air campaign over Germany, Invasion of Sicily, Italy, invasion of North Africa, South Vietnam, and North Vietnam.

Currently he is president of Port Dixie Imports, Inc., one of the largest importers of Australian and Chilean wine into the US. In 1943 he married Geraldine, 1st Lt, USAF flight nurse of the 806th Air Evacuation Squadron-England, who passed away in January 1992. Vito remarried in 1993 to Merrie Davis-Pedone who is currently the publisher of *In New York* magazine. He has been a member of the Boy Scouts of America since 1937, holds the rank of Eagle Scout and is a member of the BASA Silver Beaver Order.

He has one son Lt. Col. Stephen P. Pedone, USAF (Ret.); three grandchildren (Lisa, Michelle and Stephen); and three great-grandchildren (Kristen, Ashley and David).

Col. Pedone's military ratings as command pilot, and parachutist and received the Legion of Merit, DFC, Air Medal w/5 clusters, Unit Citation and the ETO Ribbon w/3 Arrowheads and two clusters.

He is an original member of the 9th Air Force Association's Board of Directors.

BERNARD PETROSKY, Sergeant, born in Luzerne, PA and spent his first 18 years in Pennsylvania. Then he had an offer to travel and signed up with Uncle Sam in September 1942. Travel was not first class and the trains were smoky and packed. His state room had a hundred soldiers for one bathroom. Basic training was 10 days in a hotel in Florida cleaning bathrooms.

Went to Armament School at Lowry Field, Denver, CO; to Yale to teach at the college, where he taught synchronizing the guns on P-39s; to Tallahoma, TN to 48th FBG, put in the 495th and later assigned to the 494th where he stayed until discharged.

After several months they were sent to Camp Shanks and boarded the *Queen Mary,* landed in Scotland and took a train to base at Ibsley. After D-Day they went to their new home A-4 to get ready for the rest of the group.

Memorable Experiences: on a training mission they were to go on maneuvers via C-47 and were bumped by a colonel, so had to go in tail of B-26 (was that ever cold); also memorable was D-Day and watching the planes going over like a blackbird migration in fall.

They moved often to new fields following the Army in France, Belgium and Germany. After almost two years in Europe, they took a holiday to the Rivera. They were waiting for orders to go to the Pacific when Japan surrendered. They came home on a troop ship, and he was discharged in September 1945 from Indiantown Gap, PA, and returned to Minneapolis.

Married 57 years, he has three children and five grandchildren. He drove a truck hauling freight and mail and did some long distance runs and also worked in construction as a driver hauling heavy machines. He likes to fish, garden, travel, and go to reunions.

ISAAC GALE PHILLIPS, First Lieutenant, born in Clark County, KS, on March 16, 1922. He graduated from Ashland High School, Ashland, KS in May 1941. He joined the USAAC on Sept. 28, 1942 in California.

He was sent to Class C-3, Flight Eleven, 90th College Training Detachment at Oklahoma A&M,

Stillwater, OK; then to the School of Aviation Cadets at Pine Bluff, AK. After completing this training, he was sent to Moore Field, Class 44-C, J Flight, for Advanced Flying School. He finished on March 12, 1944.

He departed the USA aboard the *Queen Mary* bound for England. Arriving in Mons, Belgium, he was assigned on Nov. 24, 1944, to the 9th AF, 365th FG, 387th Sqdn. and flew 52 missions covering the Ardennes-Alsace, Central Europe, Normandy, northern France and the Rhineland.

Phillips was awarded the EAME Service Medal, Air Medal w/4 Bronze OLCs, DFC, two Presidential Citations and two unit awards from the Belgian army. He was discharged from service on Oct. 19, 1945.

Graduated from Chico State University, Chico, CA with a BA degree in science. He taught biology and chemistry in high school for 27 years. After retiring, he earned his contractor's license. Quitting this self-employed job, he now spends his time doing graphic art using the computer and playing golf.

In 1950 he married Marie Davis in Chico, CA. They have one son, Michael, and two granddaughters.

DONALD G. PHINNEY enlisted in USAAC in November 1942. Basic training was at Atlantic City and Burlington, NC. He saw Capt. Glen Miller's AAF orchestra often. Graduated Radio Mechanic & Operator School, Fort Monmouth, NJ in 1943. Assigned to Mitchell Field, NY and on to Kilkeel, northern Ireland with the 84th Station Compliment Sqdn. of the 8th AF Gunnery Training School.

Went to Chelmsford, England in 1944 with the 44th AF Group and reassigned to the 9th AF and the 29th Air Disarmament Sqdn. Entered Europe in late 1944 and occupied war sights in France, Schweinfurt, Poking, Erbrach and Munich Germany until late 1945.

Discharged in sergeant rating with several medals including Bronze Battle Star in early 1946. Graduated University of California and Chabot College with business administration degrees. Employed with AT&T system 36 years as production and inspector - buyer positions.

Married since 1947, he has six children and nine grandchildren. Retired in Sun City Roseville, CA.

RICHARD H. PIERCE, a cavalry ROTC and CPT student at UMASS, was commissioned in May 1942 and graduated US Cavalry School, Fort Riley, KS. Transferred to flight training with many who preferred planes to tanks.

Married Constance Bookman of Philadelphia and Kansas City and chose Primary at Spartan School of Aeronautics in December 1942. Graduated 43-F, Moore Field, TX, and assigned C-47 transition, Bergstrom Field, Austin, TX. From the troop carrier replacement pool, he flew in the stream of C-47s to England in December 1943, then assigned to 76th TCS.

Flew in all six European invasions, D-Day to Rhine Crossing, earning the Air Medal w/6 OLCs and DUC. The 76th departed France to Fort Wayne, IN in July 1945, awaiting redeployment to Pacific. Separated from service in September 1945 and joined USAFR at General Spaatz Field, Reading, PA in C-46s.

Retired from PQ Corporation, Valley Forge, PA, after 36 years as Senior R&D Chemist. He and Constance had three children and three grandchildren.

WILLIAM E. "BILL" PLUMMER, born June 16, 1924 in Raeford, NC and entered the USAAC Dec. 9, 1942 as a private. He finished Aerial Gunnery School in February 1943 as a sergeant. Entered Cadets April 7, 1943 and finished March 11, 1944 as second lieutenant.

After flying P-47s at Goldsboro, NC and Wilmington, NC, and having had two walk-away engine failures, he was in Shrewsbury, England for a month, a week in Paris, to Rheims to join the 362nd FG and on to Verdun. He had another walk-away crash in a corn field on take-off, fully loaded with a belly tank of gas and two 1,000 pound bombs when one wheel broke off after hitting an AA search light.

He was a forward air controller, 16th Armd. Div., April 5, 1945 to end of war in Pilsen, Czechoslovakia. A memorable experience was shooting down a Focke-Wulf 190. He flew 88 combat missions (no military heroics) and received all the usual Battle Stars and campaign ribbons and Air Medals. He turned 21 in Paris on his way home. His final rank was first lieutenant.

Married Mary Saidla while at Auburn University where he got his doctor of veterinary medicine degree in June 1950. His practice from then to present is in Goldsboro. Bill and Mary are the parents of three sons and one daughter. They also have eight grandchildren and five great-grandchildren.

HENRY J. POCHILY was called to active duty on Feb. 21, 1943 at Atlantic City, NJ. After attending

CTD and Pre-Flight School, he started pilot training at Dorr Field in Arcadia, FL as a member of Class 44-D. He graduated from Advanced Flight School and received his wings and a commission as a 2nd lieutenant at Marianna, FL on April 15, 1944.

After transitional training in P-40s, he transferred to Blackstone, VA to start training in P-47s after which he received further Thunderbolt instruction at Seymour Johnson Field, Goldsboro, NC and Dover AFB, Dover, DE. Joined the 377th Sqdn. of the 362nd FG of the 9th AF at Etain, France. He flew his first of 79 missions on Dec. 8, 1944, shortly before the Battle of the Bulge. At a former German AFB in Frankfurt, Germany, he completed his last combat mission on April 27, 1945

For his military service he was awarded the Air Medal w/14 OLCs, the Distinguished Unit Citation and the European Theatre Ribbon w/3 Battle Stars. Returned to the USA in August 1945 and was discharged from Fort Dix, NJ on Oct. 30, 1945. Prior to discharge he was a 1st lieutenant.

After discharge he returned to work in the engineering department of an electric utility and retired as a operations supervisor in 1987. Married to the former MaryAnn Behil since 1948, he has three children and seven grandchildren.

GEORGE PULLIS, Captain, Murphysboro, IL. He was drafted into the Armed Forces Oct. 13, 1942, and reported to the classification center, Camp Grant, IL. He was assigned to the USAAC and sent to Miami Beach for basic training. While in basic training he applied for and was accepted in the Cadet Flight Training program; upon completion he was ordered to the Classification

Center at Nashville, where he was assigned to pilot training and ordered to pre-flight training at Montgomery, AL.

After completing pilot training at Napier Field in the Class of 43-J, he was assigned to the Eastern Training Command for transition training in the P-47 Thunderbolt. He completed P-47 training at Seymour Johnson Field; departed Boston March 17, 1943; arriving in the ETO, and reported to the 48th FG, 493rd FS, 9th AF, Ibsley.

He flew 113 missions in six ETO campaigns and was awarded the campaign medal w/6 Bronze Stars, Air Medal w/18 OLCs, DFC, DUB, Victory Medal and the Belgian Fourragere. He was discharged at Scott Field, IL Jan. 16, 1946.

Completed a master's degree and was a teacher and counselor for 34 years. He is now retired. His life has been one fantastic flight.

RALPH R. RAGASE, Corporal, born Feb. 5, 1923, Steubenville, OH. He served in the military Feb. 12, 1943 to Sept. 10, 1945 and served with the 377th FS, 362nd FG in communication.

Memorable experiences include first shelling in Normandy (A-12 Balleroe France) on July 2, 1944, from a hill two miles away –

two good men were lost that night; in Rennes A-27, Aug. 10, 1944 when they were strafed by a single plane along runway and one guy jumped into an open latrine.

His awards include the Good Conduct, two Presidential Citations, four Bronze Stars, EAME Campaign and WWII Victory Medal.

Married to Dorothy Phillips for 34 years. Family includes two sons, Joe and Dave; two grandsons, Daniel and Mark; two granddaughters, Karie and Christy, one great-grandson, Justin Wagner; two stepsons, Bob and Jim Mayhugh; one stepdaughter, Hope Ann Mayhugh. Ralph retired after 34 years as a machinist.

STEVE RAMBERT, born July 19, 1921, Chicago, IL. Enlisted in the USAAC and went to McChord Field. Assigned to the 83rd Sqdn., 12th BG, Earthquaker, and went to Esler Field, LA, then to Las Vegas Gunnery School and on July 3, 1942 to Fort Dix, NY.

On July 15, 1942 he departed on USS *Louis Pasteur* for Egypt. He survived two crashes, 7th mission on Oct. 27 and 8th mission on Oct. 29, 1942. Participated in all the battles in Egypt, Libya, Tunisia,

Panterella, Sicily and Italy.

Credited with 55 missions, he received the Air Medal w/4 OLCs, four Battle Stars and DUC. Returned to the States Oct. 24, 1943, sent to Mather Field, CA, 1944 and to Douglas Field in Arizona where he was discharged Sept. 20, 1945 with the rank of staff sergeant.

After 20 years with Prudential Ins., he retired and is now enjoying life.

EUGENE D. REAVES, Sergeant, born March 12, 1922 at Foreman, AR. He joined the service in September 1942 with basic training at Keesler Field, MS; Aircraft Armament School at Buckley Field, CO and graduated in January 1943 to Westover Field, Springfield, MA.

Assigned to the 362nd FG, March 1943; November-July 1943 in England; and July 1944-August 1945 in France. Soon after arriving in France, the 362nd Gp. received many combat experiences: being shelled with German heavy artillery, the many bombing raids, mortar and small arms fire. He soon learned to move away from apple orchards and go underground in fox holes (some of which were quite deep and quite elaborate) where he felt much safer. He remembers being strafed by enemy aircraft, threatened by "Axis Sally," Germany's female propagandist and broadcast person.

Processed in Southern France, given summer clothes and gear and many tropical shots and shipped out of Marseilles in August 1945. After a few days out the PA system on ship announced that Hiroshima, Japan, had been dealt a death blow with the first atom bomb. There was much celebrating aboard ship and they changed course for Hampton Roads, VA.

He was discharged from service in September 1945.

NAT C. RHINEHART, born Nov. 21, 1916, in Jena, LA. Enlisted in USAAC Aug. 16, 1942 and served with the 379th FS for three and a half years. Two were spent in the European Theater. His rank was staff sergeant, and he was a crew chief on a plane piloted by Lt. Marvin Swafford.

His awards were Good Conduct Medal, and Unit Citation w/ OLC. Upon his discharge on Sept. 9, 1945 he worked for Armco Steel as Plant Superintendent for 32 years. Retired in 1972 and passed away with heart attack on Oct. 3, 1989.

Married for 43 years to the former Dorothy Kuhn, they had four children, eight grandchildren and five great-grandchildren.

BOB & DICK RICHARDS, as either a past president or reunion chairman of the P-47 Thunderbolt Pilots Assn., Bob has observed and enjoyed many get-togethers of long lost war buddies. Bob was a child of divorce, his dad went on to start another family and Dick was sent to boarding school.

In the Fall of 1942 Dick Richards (42 years old) and his son Bob enlisted in the USAAC (without each other's knowledge). Dick was eventually assigned to the 391st BG, 573rd BS (B-26) and shipped to England as a first sergeant. Bob graduated at Napier Field as a SE pilot, was held over as an instrument instructor, and later sent to join the 373rd FG, 411th FS in P-47s.

Bob and Dick were able to meet on three occasions and cement a father-son bond that lasted until Dick's death in 1964. Bob is sure that they were the only enlisted father/son in the 9th (or even the USAAC) serving during the war and especially where the son outranked his dad. It did not, however, change the pecking order!

FREDERICK W. RINGGER JR., born July 9, 1922 in Baltimore, MD. He was inducted into USAAC March 22, 1943. After basic training in Miami Beach, FL, he trained at Keesler Field, MS, then to Weather School

at Chanute Field, IL. Before completing this training, he was sent to England to prepare for Normandy landings for the invasion of Europe.

Assigned to 49th Mobile Reclamation and Repair Squadron, 9th AF, at Chalgrove. Shortly after June 6, 1944 they landed at Omaha Beach to support Gen. George Patton's 3rd Army drive through France and Germany. Assigned as engineering specialist to help keep the planes "in the air" supporting the ground forces assaulting the German army. His unit received the Army Meritorious Unit Citation and was awarded four Battle Stars.

Served as sergeant in the Army Occupation of Germany before returning to the States Dec. 24, 1945 at Camp Patrick Henry, Newport News, VA. He was honorably discharged Dec. 31, 1945.

Attended Johns Hopkins University Night School and accepted a position with the Baltimore County Department of Public Works Engineering Department and retired after 36 years. Married to the former Alice M. Lochner since 1946. They have four children and six grandchildren.

HARRY C. ROGAL, First Lieutenant, graduated from Aviation Cadets, Class 43-E, Moore Field, TX; P-47 training as Charter Member 388th FG, Westover, MA.

Assigned to 9th AF, 368th FG, Chilbolton, England; Omaha Beach, France; and Normandy Invasion. He  flew air cover for Gen. Patton's 3rd Army. Completed 86 missions and received the DFC, Air Medal w/13 OLCs and PUC.

He was a flight instructor multi engine and instruments, Air Force Reserve, Scott Field, IL, through 1948, while attending Parks Air College, Cahokia, IL.

Executive pilot 25 years (16 @ LGA) he accumulated 25,000 accident free hours before retiring in January 1990. Celebrated 59th wedding anniversary on June 4, 2002. Now residing at Palm Beach Gardens, FL.

MARVIN J. ROSVOLD enlisted in USAAC in July 1941; graduated Air Mechanics School, Chanute Field, IL in 1942 and entered Aviation Cadets in September 1942 with Class 43-E. Commissioned May 24, 1943 at Aloe Field, Victoria, TX and assigned to Westover Field for P-47 training.

Transferred to the 368th FG to England and the 9th AF with combat operations from Greenham Common. Downed by gunfire on the 65th mission, he was able to rejoin  the squadron to complete 12 additional trips, totaling 77.

Decorated with DFC, Purple Heart, Air Medal w/13 OLCs, and the DUC. In 1944 he returned to the US and was fighter gunnery instructor at Page Field until discharged in October 1945.

Rosvold is a graduate of North Dakota State University having earned a bachelor of architecture degree. He operates a private architectural practice. Married to the former Geraldine Benson since 1947, they have five children, 14 grandchildren, and six great-grandchildren.

CLIFFORD R. SAARI, born June 6, 1922 in Ironwood, MI. Enlisted in the USAAC Sept. 10, 1942 and went on active duty Feb. 23, 1943. Entered Aviation Cadets May 23 1943 and graduated with class 44-C March 18, 1944  from Eagle Pass, TX. Assigned to 1st AF in Richmond, VA and began P-47 training. Received more training at Camp Springs and Millville, NJ and shipped to England Sept. 23, 1944.

Assigned to 378th FS, 362nd FG, Nov. 1, 1944 in Reims, France; also flew from Etain, France, Frankfurt Germany and Illsheim, Germany. Flew 80 combat missions and received the Air Medal w/13 OLCs and DUC. Discharged Nov. 28, 1945 as 1st lieutenant from Santa Anna AB, CA.

Graduate of Superior State Teachers College, Superior, WI with BS degree and University of Wisconsin Madison, WI with MS degree. Taught math and chemistry and coached football in high school. Retired in 1984 as an administrator from West High School in Green Bay, WI.

KEMAL SAIED, born Nov. 22, 1919, Healdton, OK. Attended Classen High School, Oklahoma City and University of Oklahoma. Enlisted in the USAAC in August 1941. After attaining the rank of staff sergeant, he entered Aviation Cadet training, graduating with Class 43-J at Luke Field, AZ. After instructing over five months in basic training, he requested combat flying P-47s, and assigned to the 404th FG, 508th Sqdn. in Europe.

He accumulated 62 combat missions and was awarded the DFC, Purple Heart and Air Medal w/7 OLCs. The 404th FG was awarded the DUC, Belgian Fourragere and the French Croix de Guerre w/Palm. He left the service in November 1945.

In 1989, he authored a book titled, *Thunderbolt Odyssey: P-47 War In Europe,* that describes the life and experiences of a combat P-47 pilot in Europe.

RALPH L. SALLEE, Captain, born 1922 in Hollywood, CA. He worked for Lockheed Aircraft building Loadstar and P-38 in 1941. Enlisted in Air Corps in 1942 and called in February 1943.

Commissioned 2nd lieutenant Feb. 8, 1944, Luke Field, AZ and honored for exceptional air gunnery at graduation and received extra set of wings.

Trained in P-40 and P-47 and shipped to England for final training preparation for invasion. Flown to first field on invasion strip and looked for and found where their field (A-12) was to be built.

He lived in fox holes with buddies, Percy and Plochere, in hedge row. Occasionally shelled, bombed once, and watched Howitzer fire daily. Attached to 362nd FG, 379th FS as replacement and started flying combat as soon as the field was finished and the group moved in.

He flew 100 missions, then volunteered to be forward controller for the 80th Inf. Div. until V-E Day. Decorations included DFC, Air Medal w/19 OLCs, two DUCs and A P-38 Pistol (Patton saw that high mission pilots received it).

Ralph's personal pride exists in the daily help that his squadron gave their Infantry and Tankers in the "Bulge" in spite of great losses. Also, in air-to-air combat when leading a cover flight on Dec. 26, 1944 spotting and "calling in" 35 enemy planes attacking their ground troops.

With team work, their two flights (8 Thunderbolts) were able to knock down a total of nine FW-190s with only the loss of Red Leader who belly landed within their lines.

After V-J Day he married Harriett R. and had two sons. He worked at Aerojet on first Satellite rocket (LH2 and 02 in 1947). Howard Hughes (Falcon Missile) and Air Research on gas turbines. Retired in 1960 and moved to Hawaii.

RANDALL E. SANDERS, Tech Sergeant, born Jan. 6, 1923, Chandler, IN, Warrick County. He joined the service in February 1943 and served with 362nd FG, 378th FS, Ordnance section.

Discharged in September 1945, his awards include the DUC w/cluster and six Battle Stars.

Married Ruth Mottler on Oct. 29, 1943 and they have two daughters, Randa Kaye Sanders and Judith Ann Crom. In the trucking and excavating business, 1946-72 and ready mix concrete business, 1955 to 1989 when he sold out and retired.

L. GENE SIDWELL, Colonel, born March 7, 1918. He lived in Iowa City, IA where he attended grade school, junior high and a year of high school. His mother died when he was 11 and his father when he was 16. He next attended Villisca, Iowa High School and later graduated from Halsey High School in Nebraska. He entered the State University of Iowa in 1935 and immediately became interested in the ROTC program and the Pershing Rifles Drill Squad. After completing two years of college he then enlisted in Troop F of the 14th Cavalry at Fort Des Moines, IA in July 1938.

He returned to cattle ranching in the Nebraska Sandhills until February 1941 when he was called to active duty as a second lieutenant with Co. F of the 168th Inf. of the Iowa National Guard. They were sent to Camp Claiborne, LA for training. He completed the Infantry Company Officers Course at Fort Benning, GA, entered pilot training in June 1942 and was subsequently assigned to MacDill AFB where the 394th BG was activated in March 1943. Served as the 587th Squadron Operations Officer and subsequently as Group Operations Officer of the 394th BG. Received promotions of captain, major and lieutenant colonel.

After WWII he received a regular commission, graduated from the Air Command and Staff School and later was assigned to Strategic Air Command serving eight years. For three years they were at MacDill AFB where he was the commander of the 368th BS (B-29), executive officer of the 306th BG, and later the Operations Officer for the 6th Air Div. Their next station was Lake Charles, LA where he was the deputy group commander for the 68th BW. Transferred to Offutt AFB, NE for three years where he was the deputy director of personnel for SAC.

He graduated from the Air War College at Maxwell AFB, AL in 1957, then assigned to the Pentagon for three years. He was chief of USAF Enlisted Assignment Division which required the formulation of policy, procedures and control for 600,000 enlisted personnel and warrant officers. Earned a BS in commerce, University of Iowa; MA in personnel management, George Washington University, DC.

Credited with 49 missions, WWII, as pilot of a B-26. His awards include the DFC, Air Medal w/Silver and 8 OLCs, DUB French Croix de Guerre with Etoile de Vermeil, Commendation Ribbon (SAC HQ) and various Campaign Ribbons. Voluntary retirement May 31, 1960 after 21 years of active service. His rank is Colonel, USAF.

He met his future wife, Laura Lee Lane, a native of Tampa, FL, where they were married in 1943. She made the changes of stations with the group to Ardmore, OK and Battle Creek, MI. She returned to Tampa and worked for the Tampa Electric Co. while he was overseas for 18 months. Laura Lee, was very active in the "Grey Lady Program" in the hospitals at MacDill AFB and Offutt AFB. Subsequently three boys and one girl were born, all have college degrees, all are married and have children. Two of the boys, Gregory and Michael received commissions in the Army Signal Corps and both have now retired.

After retiring from the Air Force, he returned to cattle ranching in Nebraska, then worked for the Lockheed-Georgia Co. for over eight years in configuration management of C-5 airplane program. Laura Lee, has been busy all of this time keeping up with family needs and meeting aggravations of moving to locations where we purchased seven different homes. So much for the availability of "Government Family Quarters!" We finally "stabilized" and have been in Georgia for 37 years.

Now retired and active in the community. He serves or has served on the Board of Directors, Georgia Genealogical Society; past treasurer of Cobb County, GA, Genealogical Society; past treasurer of Friends of National Archives; past treasurer and secretary of Northwest Unitarian Church, and currently president, 384th BG Assn. (B-26).

ALAN M. SILVERBACH, Lieutenant Colonel, joined the 1st Inf. Div. as a 2nd lieutenant in January 1942 and became an international diplomatic courier (probably carrying Mrs. Roosevelt's secret recipes to Mrs. Churchill), transferred to the  Air Corps and graduated Class of 43-F. Silverbach graduated from New York Military Academy in 1939, and attended Duke University Class 1943.

Requested B-26s and joined the 397th BG, 598th Sqdn. at MacDill, FL. As a first pilot, they flew their own planes via Brazil, Ascension Island, Africa to England, and from there flew missions including D-Day. They were shot down over France, crashed on one of a few US fighter strips and all escaped unharmed. Then with the group moved to various airfields in France.

Flew 65 missions, received the DFC, Air Medal w/12 clusters and various unit citations. Returned to States at end of 1944, attended Adjutant Generals School and helped set up the Separation and Counseling Center at Hunter Field. Retired as a lieutenant colonel.

Joined 20th Century-Fox in 1946 and headed their Television Distribution Co. throughout the world. Formed an independent TV company in 1976 and am still playing at it. Married the former Meredith Lang and they have one son and three grandchildren.

JACK E. SMITH, born Dec. 29, 1921 in Middletown, OH. In April 1942, Jack enlisted in the USAAC while working at Fairfield Air Depot Patterson Field, Dayton, OH. He was assigned to the newly formed 316th TCG, 456th TCS. After training, the group headed overseas in November 1942.  Upon arrival in Egypt, they were assigned to the 12th AF, and later, the 9th AF for the remainder of the war in Europe.

He took part in five major invasions during 30 months of overseas duty. Jack was a tech sergeant crew chief on C-47 aircraft. His military decorations include the Air Medal w/2 OLCs, DUC w/2 OLCs and European Theater Ribbon w/9 Battle Stars. The group's last base was RAF Station 489 Cottesmore, England.

Returned to the States after V-E Day and stationed at Pope Field, NC until the end of WWII. He was discharged in September 1945.

After some schooling, he joined a heavy construction company in engineering. Later, he transferred to Armco Steel Co. in engineering until retirement in 1990. Married since 1952 to the former Mary Lou Leight, they have two children and three granddaughters.

CASIMIER V. "SLIM" SOCHOCKI, born Jan. 28, 1923, enlisted in the USAAC Jan. 16, 1942 and sworn in at Fort Benjamin Harrison, IN. He was attached to the 303rd FG for the first eight months, transferred in grade in September 1942 to the 453rd BS, 323rd BG.

Went overseas aboard the *Queen Elizabeth* and debarked at Gourock, Scotland at the Firth of Clyde on May 11, 1942. Stationed at Horham Field in England until June 13   when they moved to Earls Colne. The 323rd BG pulled their first mission July 16, 1943. He was section chief of the Ordnance until he started flying as toggleer on Dec. 24, 1944. He flew 34 missions over France, Belgium, Holland and Germany. Of the 45 months he spent in service, 30 months of them was overseas.

He was discharged Oct. 9, 1945 with 124 points as a technical sergeant. He received the Air Medal w/ 5 OLCs.

After discharge he was a machinist for three years, then became a professional truck driver and drove for 34 years, retiring at the age of 59. At present he is doing custom cabinet making.

Married Dorothy in July 1947 and they have a daughter, son, granddaughter and two great-grandchildren.

HARRY C. SORENSEN, Major, USAF (Ret.), born Feb. 1, 1922, Kennard, NE. Locations include April-October 1942, Wright-Patterson AFB; October 1942-January 1943, Hondo, TX; January-February 1943, Chanute Field, IL; February 1943, Salt Lake City, UT, AAB; 398th BG, 600th Sqdn., 8th AF; October 1943, Rapid City, SD, 8th AF.

Overseas locations: December 1943-June 1944, 9th AF, England; June 1944, Omaha Beach; 9th AF, 31st MR&R; January 1944-April 1945, 41st MR&R; Air Disarm Log (Prov) German air force; October 1945, HQ and Base Service Sqdn. 485th AC Gp.; October 1945, 902nd Engr. Sqdn.; October-November 1945, Dep. A 43rd Air Dep. Rep. Sqdn.; November 1945-February 1946, 30th Dep. Rep. Sqdn.

Returned to the USA, February-March 1946; Joined the USAFR in March 1946 and recalled 1950-53 for Korean War. Returned to AF Reserve units and retired. He went through all ratings from private to major, April 1942-April 2002, 60 years of continuous service.

CHARLES C. STANDRING, Master Sergeant, born April 21, 1919, Cleveland, OH. Served in the 112th OBS Sqdn., Cleveland, OH; 118th OBS Sqdn., Langley Field, VA; USAF HQ&HQ, Bolling Field, Washington, DC; April 1942, HQ&HQ, 9th AAF, Bolling Field, Washington, DC.

Served with 9th AF Service Command, Oct. 15, 1943,

Altermasten, England as CO, pilot on C-47, aerial engineer, AAF technical inspector. Discharged in October 1945, Sanata, CA.

His memorable experiences were trouble shooting airplanes that wouldn't start on Omaha Beach and building a canvas hangar to repair C-47s at C-81 strip in France. He retired from General Motors Corp. with 33 years service. He has five children and 12 grandchildren.

ISADOR "IZZY" STEINER, enlisted in the USAAF in August 1942 in Pittsburgh, PA. When his birth certificate was presented, it was Isaac so his military records are Isaac. He was airplane armorer with campaigns in Normandy, Northern France, Rhineland, Ardennes and Central Europe.

Transferred to Group Headquarters 379th Sqdn., was musician in Nelson GaNuns Band. Highest rank was staff sergeant, 362d FG, 9th AF. Discharged in September 1945. He earned DUC w/OLC and EAME Medal w/6 Bronze Stars.

Elected to Port Vue Borough Council and served 37 years as president of Allegheny County Boroughs Assn., president of Pennsylvania State Assn. of Boroughs and received the Excellence in Local Government Award from Governor. Retired from Allegheny County Property Assessment Appeals and Review Board.

Izzy died March 22, 2002 at age 78. He is survived by wife June, sons James and Daniel, and five granddaughters.

GEORGE L. SUTCLIFFE, born in North Providence, RI. He graduated in Class 43-E from Moore Field, Mission, TX and was commissioned in May 1943. He was assigned to 368th FG at Westover Field, MA for P-47 training.

Arrived in England in January 1944. Group was assigned to 9th AF. George flew 80 missions escorting bombers, dive-bombing and ground support. His awards include the Silver Star, DFC, Air Medal w/12 clusters and DUC.

Returned to States in November 1944 and instructed Aviation Cadets at Luke Field, AZ and instructed combat tactics in P-51 at Punta Gorda, FL. Also flew F-86 in USAFR.

Discharged from service in October 1945. Graduated from Bryant College with degree in accounting and finance. He owned and operated Independent Insurance Agency for 40 years.

George and his wife Olive celebrated 57th wedding anniversary in November 2001. They have a daughter Lynne, son Barry, and five grandsons.

OSCAR E. THEIS, born Jan. 6, 1920, enlisted in USAAC in November 1939 at Randolph Field, San Antonio, TX and served there for three years as aircraft mechanic and crew chief. Achieved rank of staff sergeant and entered enlisted pilot training, Class 42-K, and appointed flight officer on Dec. 9, 1942. Trained flexible gunners at Las Vegas Flexible Gunnery School, Las Vegas, NV for one year. Entered P-47 pilot training at Richmond, VA in January 1944.

Arrived in England in May 1944 and was assigned to the 405th FG, 509th Sqdn. as a replacement pilot. Flew 117 combat missions. Squadron operations officer. He flew surrendered German FW-190 fighter. Decorations include the DFC w/OLC, Air Medal w/19 OLCs, DUC, ETO Medal w/6 Battle Stars. Retired from USAFR as lieutenant colonel.

Retired from farming and ranching in Texas, he attends the yearly 405th Fighter Group reunions and does RV traveling. Married to the former Iris Melde in May 1946, they have three children and six grandchildren. Iris passed away in 1992 and he married Elsie Terry in 1997.

JULIAN DWAINE THWING, enlisted in the USAAC Aviation Cadet program in November 1942. Assigned to Class 44-B at Santa Ana, CA and received his wings and commission in February 1944 at Williams Field, Chandler, AZ. P-47 training was at Blackstone, VA and Dover, DE.

Assigned to 9th AF, 362nd FG, 379th Sqdn. in Headcorn, England on July 1, 1944. The group moved to France on July 15, 1944 and 91 combat missions were flown to war's end. Primarily dive-bombing, strafing and close support operations during Patton's march across Europe.

Awarded the Air Medal w/16 OLCs and DUC w/OLC. Returned to the States in May 1945 and married former Helen Barnum in September 1945. They have three children and seven grandchildren. Thwing held executive management positions in finance and administration with radio and electronics manufacturers until his retirement in 1978.

FREDERICK W. "MIKE" TURNER, born May 13, 1923 and loved to ski. His love of sailing through the air on a pair of ski's soon brought him to even greater heights as a fighter pilot. This journey began with his enlistment at Fort Devens, MA. He attended AAF training and Lodwick Aviation Military Academy, graduating in November 1943.

Commissioned as a second lieutenant in the USAAC at Marianna Air Base in Florida, he soon joined other newly trained pilots in the air over Germany. He flew with the 377th FS where he was credited with destroying one ME-109 in the air and four enemy planes on the ground. Shot down on his 81st mission over Czechoslovakia and reported "missing in action" he walked 150 miles, until he was picked up by a section of Patton's Fourth Armd. Div.

He received The EAME Theater Ribbon w/3 Battle Stars, Air Medal w/15 OLCs, Good Conduct Medal, Overseas Service Bar and DFC. He was honorably discharged as 1st lieutenant in December 1945.

His love of flying is still with him, he went on to enlist in the MAANG 102nd FG. On May 24th the P-80 jet plane he was piloting crashed while on a dive bombing run at Eglin Field, FL. He was 28 years old.

He was survived by his wife, Jean, and two daughters, Janice and Lucinda. Out of the eight grandchildren that came later, one is a pilot, one is in the Army and one loves to ski.

JOHN V. TWYMAN, born 1919 in London and moved to New York in 1935. Went to high school, attended New York University (engineering), 1938-40, and worked at Wall Street Bank until 1941.

Enlisted in the USAAC in January 1942 at Fort Dix, NY and served with West Coast Flying Training Command, 4th AF, USSTAF and IX AF Service Command, 30th Air Depot Group. He had administrative jobs at Lemoore AAF, CA, 1942-44, reaching rank of tech sergeant. Shipped to England in February 1945; administrative work at USSTAF RAF Uxbridge until V-E Day, Control Amber 1 Airway, London-Paris.

Transferred to continent in June 1945, 9th AF HQ, 391st BG, 394th BG, 97th BW until V-J Day; 303rd Sta. Comp. Sq., Illesheim, Germany, arranging for shipment of high-point men to US, September-December 1945; 303rd Sta. Comp. Sq., Furstenfeldbruck, Germany, as casual, 1945-46; transferred to Fort Dix by way of Camp Tophat, Antwerp and Camp Kilmer, NJ.

Discharged in February 1946, his awards include the Good Conduct Medal, American Theater, ETO, Victory, Occupation Service Medals and Carbine Expert Badge.

Enrolled at UCLA on GI Bill in September 1946 and graduated in January 1950. Employed by Pennzoil Co., 1952-67 in advertising production and operated own visual-aids-for-education business, 1951 to date.

Married since 1955, they live in Hollywood, CA.

PAUL L. VAN CLEEF, born April 6, 1921, Salina, KS, enlisted April 1, 1942 in USAAC as Aviation Cadet, Fort Riley, KS. Flight training at Maxwell Field, Montgomery, AL; Avon Park, FL: Shaw Field, Sumter, NC; Spence Field, Moultrie, GA, 1942-43. Commissioned Spence Field, GA, May 28, 1943, Class of 43-E. Transitioned to P-47 Bird Field, Richmond, VA, 1943 in newly formed 365th FG, 387th FS.

Deployed with Group 13 December 1943 to Gosfield, England, 9th AF, ETO, then to Beaulieu,

England, March 1944. Participated in D-Day invasion. Moved to Strip A-7, Sur Mere Eglise, Normandy, France, June 28, 1944, then Belgium and Germany to end of war. He flew 110 combat missions, 240 combat hours in P-47.

Awards included DFC, Belgian Croix de Guerre (2), Belgian Fourragere, Air Medal w/17 clusters, Air Force Commendation Medal, ETO Ribbon w/6 Battle Stars, Distinguished Unit Citation w/cluster, Korean Service Medal, UN Service Medal w/Bronze OLC, WWII Victory Medal and American Theater Ribbon.

Returned to States in June 1945 and remained in Air Force including one year as primary flight instructor, Goodfellow Field, San Angelo, TX; in Comptroller Field, two four-year tours, Germany and France; two four-year tours at the Pentagon; two year tour on Okinawa, HQ 20th Air Force; and a four year tour as executive officer, AFROTC, Purdue University. Retired in 1971 as lieutenant colonel.

Graduate of University of Maryland. Married former Dorothy L. Wells in 1943; they have four children, six grandchildren and six great-grandchildren. Retired Lafayette, IN, 1971 to present.

KENNETH H. WEBER, First Lieutenant, born May 26, 1923, Covington, NY and drafted into service on Jan. 13, 1943. Sent to Fort Niagara, NY; Fort Eustes, VA for antiaircraft 40mm training; and Radio School.

Went to Nashville, TN for test and made pilot, then to Montgomery, AL for preflight; Orangeburg, SC for primary; Sumter, SC for basic; and Moultrie, GA for advanced; graduated and flew 10 hours in P-40 and P-47 at Blackstone, VA.

Went overseas and joined the 362nd FG at Headcorn, England then on to France and Germany. He flew 90 missions. His decorations include the Air Medal w/3 OLCs, ETO w/5 stars, Jubilee of Victory for D-Day and Unit Citation, OLC. He was discharged Aug. 11, 1945.

Worked for an oil company for 46 years, retiring May 31, 1988. He has been married 57 years and has four children.

RALPH M. WEFEL, as a staff sergeant radio-operator aerial gunner, he flew 26 missions over Germany in the Martin B-26 Marauder twin-engine medium bomber. In 1942 he enlisted in Cleveland, OH, as an Air Force Reserve Aviation Cadet Candidate.

This allowed him to return to his college studies at Miami University of Ohio until called to service in 1943. Following basic training with 1,000 other USAAC Aviation Cadet Candidates at Keesler Field, Biloxi, MS, he completed additional college training studies at the Drake University CTD (College Training Detachment), Des Moines, IA. At Santa Anna AFB (SAAFB) in California, failure of the questionable depth perception eye exam ended his Aviation Cadet dreams.

After the end of WWII, he studied architecture under the GI Bill of Rights at his former Miami University of Ohio in Oxford, OH; culminating in a BArch degree in 1950 from the School of Architecture of the University of Southern California, Los Angeles, CA. He is now a licensed Architect-Retired, state of California.

In 1952-53 with his first wife, he traveled around the world in 13 months working as an architect in Karachi, Pakistan; Tokyo, Japan; and Honolulu, HI. His architectural career has included the design of nuclear electrical power plants; USAAF IRBM and ICBM Ballistic Missile launch sites; management of USN missile test facilities; project architecture and construction management. In retirement his hobbies are Wefel Family Genealogy and HTML computer design of Internet Web Sites. His own WEFEL and Ralph's WWII USAAF Martin B-36 Marauder info Web Page is at: http://www.mind.net/rmwefel/index.html.

CHARLES M. WEILAND, PFC, born Oct. 26, 1918 in Elroy, WI and born to Eternal Life, Dec. 14, 2001, Marshfield, WI. Enlisted in the USAAC, Jan. 3, 1942 and was a medic attached to the 368th FG, 396th FS. He received an honorable discharge Sept. 30, 1945.

My name is Kevin, Charles's youngest son, and I am writing this autobiography in honor of my dad. I don't have any war stories from my dad just a silence during those many years since WWII. He never really talked about the war much as I was growing up even though I was fascinated by the subject. We would watch old war movies together, only to turn my back from the TV to see his easy chair empty. Recently, with the release of *Saving Private Ryan,* I began to understand his feelings. The utter chaos, confusion, life... the struggle to hold on to it, and the suffering in between the ultimate sacrifice.

My dad disposed of most of his war memorabilia, including his medals. I guess it was a chapter in his book of life he felt he could tear out. I obtained his medals for him and presented them to him on his last birthday. He held back the tears and struggled to say, "Thank you." He relished the life he had and his family and friends, his reward was to be back home and watching his family grow. Now when I think of his silence it really spoke volumes. I can only imagine what it must have been like.

Dad, I love you and thanks to you and many more like you, I have lived my life in freedom.

EGBERT BARRON WHITE, born March 24, 1914, Memphis, TN and moved to Paducah, KY in 1923. Drafted in the US Army in November 1942; receiving basic training at Jefferson Barracks, St. Louis, MO; graduated from Aircraft Engine Mechanics School, Parks Air College, East St. Louis and accepted in OCS, Miami, FL.

Commissioned 2nd lieutenant in August 1943 and sent to Air Force School of Applied Tactics, Orlando, FL before being assigned to the 1st Air Defense Command, Philadelphia, PA.

Left the States in March 1944 and was assigned to the 303rd FW, 9th AF as fighter controller with the RAF, Biggin Hill, England. Served with the Royal Navy in the North Sea until a few weeks before D-Day. Wounded at Biggin Hill when a German V-1 bomb hit the billet on June 2, 1944. Wing moved to Normandy in July 1944. In October 1944 Wing put in XXIX Tactical Air Command.

Participated in battles at Normandy, Northern France, Ardennes, Central Europe, Air Offensive Europe and Rhineland. Discharged in October 1945 at Fort Sheridan, IL with rank of captain. Decorations include the Purple Heart, Unit Citation for Belgian Fourragere, EAME Theater Ribbon w/Silver Star and one Bronze Star.

Resumed job as salesman for Petter Supply Co., Paducah, KY, in October 1945 and retired in June 1989 after 56 years.

Married Zelma Nicholson on Aug. 10, 1957. They have two daughters, Katherine and Elizabeth. Since retirement he enjoys golf and volunteer work for Paducah Ambassadors and Paducah Rotary Club.

KENNETH L. WILCOX, First Lieutenant, born in Rutland Township, Barry County, MI March 30, 1923. Enlisted in the USAC Aug. 17, 1942 and after graduation from Aviation Cadet training, he was assigned to a single engine P-47 Training School.

Sent to England for more training, then to Normandy, France to join the 396th Sqdn. of the 368th FG on July 6, 1944. He flew 93 combat missions and received the DFC and Air Medal w/12 OLCs. Their group received the Presidential Achievement Award, French Croix de Guerre, Belgium Croix de Guerre w/palm and the Holland Orange Laniere. He was discharged Dec. 9, 1944.

His most memorable experience was his very first mission – it was a dive bomb on a bridge not far from their base, he was the leader's wingman and their No. 4 man was killed.

He has been married to Lucy Ann Brovont for 57 years and they have four children and six grandchildren. He is presently working for a pet cemetery.

JACK ARNOLD WIER, born April 29, 1917. He joined the service Jan. 7, 1942 and entered Army Cadet training at San Antonio, TX; Primary Pilot School at Tulsa, OK; BT-15s at Enid, OK and AT-6 School at San Antonio, TX. He got his wings and commission Sept. 6 (Class of 42-H).

Flew O-52s at Brooks Field, Key, FL, then to Meridan, MS for training in A-24s, V-72s, A-25s and A-36s. After crash landing of a V-72 or A-31, he lost his wings and flying status. He then served at Myrtle

Beach Walterboro, SC and Drew Field, Tampa, FL as a supply officer.

He was with 404th FG when they left New York on an old British ship for England. They went by train to Christchurch (or Winton) and their P-47s flew missions across the channel until they boarded a ship to cross the channel on or about 10 days after D-day. They walked across Omaha Beach and up the cliff, past the German cement bunkers, then walked inland until trucks caught up with them, reaching their base A-5 the next day.

At A-5 they were bombed and lost several planes and pilots. After the break through at St. Lo, they moved on up through France to Paris, to Reims, to St. Trond, Belgium, where they spent the winter months. He remembers the cold, snowy December and their planes couldn't get off to help the guys at Bastogne during the Battle of the Bulge.

They moved through many towns in Germany and finally at Antwerp by train then by Navy ship back to the States. He was discharged at Denver, CO in September 1945.

WILLIAM E. WILKERSON of Cambridge, ID, enlisted in the USAAC in August 1942, then attended Gunnery School at Fort Myers, FL and Armament School at Salt Lake City, UT. He joined the 409th BG in Oklahoma in early 1943. The 409th BG consisted of A-20 "Havoc" attack bombers which carried a crew of three, six 500- pound bombs, and nine 50 caliber machine guns.

He was the top turret gunner and flew 40 missions from the base at Sanford Waldon, England and 20 missions from the base near Paris. He flew two low-level bombing missions over Normandy on D-Day and several just prior to and after D-Day. He was awarded the Air Medal w/11 OLCs, Good Conduct Medal, EAME w/4 Battle Stars and the Medaille Du Jubilee of Freedom Medal awarded by the province of Normandy, France on the 50th anniversary of D-Day.

William returned to the States in January 1945 and became a gunnery instructor at Kingman, AZ until discharged in July 1945. He is retired in Charleston, SC with wife of 57 years and three children and five grandchildren.

DENNIS G. WILLIAMS, born Feb. 18, 1915 in the Susquehanna Valley dairy region, Unadilla, NY. Enlisted in the USAAF, May 6, 1942 at Syracuse, NY with basic training at Hunter Field, Savannah, Drew Field, Tampa and Walterboro AAB. Originally flew as rear gunner in early fighter plane. Following special training at MacDill Field, he was assigned tech sergeant, Chief of Tactical Intelligence, 405th FBG, 9th AF.

Departed New York Harbor on *Mauretania* for unescorted North Atlantic crossing to Liverpool, England. This was in February 1944 when the all time record was set for tonnage sunk by German U-boats.

Entered immediately into Air Offensive Europe upon arrival at Christchurch Airport. Next Normandy invasion and landing at Omaha Beach. During the battle of Northern France he cancelled a battlefield commission in order to remain with his group. After the Ardennes Battle of the Bulge, he entered Germany at Aachen, crossed the Rhine at Remagen, for the Rhineland campaign and on to the battle of Central Europe. After V-E Day the 405th was ordered directly on to Okinawa, cancelled by V-J Day.

Williams, now retired, was director of risk management and consultant for a Fortune 500 company. He and his wife, Dorothy, a high school sweetheart, have one son, Dennis Jr. and live in DeWitt, NY.

THOMAS A. WILLIAMS, drafted into US Army in August 1943 and assigned to Btry. D, 133rd AAA Gun Bn.(MBL) at Camp Edwards, MA, for basic and AAA training, then to Fort Bragg for advance training and anti-tank firing range.

Sent overseas to England to draw new equipment and to Utah Beach in August 1944. Assigned to 9th ADC, defense of Omaha Beach, then emplaced at St. Honorine for Cherbourg Harbor and Air Defense. Went on to Reims, Verdun and Mourmelon le Grand as air defense for 17th Abn.

operations, then to Luxembourg, Oppenheim and Bingen for air defense of Rhine crossings.

When war ended they took up occupation in Munich and Haar Germany, then Wels, Austria. They pulled in German artillery and disarmed DPs of arms they took from defeated German troops. Upon his discharge in March 1946, he enlisted in Reserves and served with 469th AW BN(Sp), 77th Inf. Div. until discharge Sept. 13, 1958 with the rank of master sergeant.

He worked 42 years for New York City Transit Authority and retired in July 1990. Married to Joan Gray who passed away Nov. 30, 1998. He has a daughter and three grandchildren.

ROLAND L. WISDOM, USAF, Major (Ret.), born July 4, 1920, Glenada, OR. Enlisted Field Artillery, 1939, and three years later graduated OCS and began pilot training. Served in the European Theater in WWII as a P-47 pilot with 362nd FG. At 6'5" he had to stoop to get into the pilot seat, earning the nickname, "Big Stoop."

Decorations include DFC w/OLC, Air Medal w/ 14 OLCs, EAME Campaign Ribbon w/4 Battle Stars, WWII Victory Medal and Presidential Unit Citation. In 1945 he was discharged but rejoined the AF and served in Air Sea Rescue Squadron in California and Bermuda.

Jet upgrade training in 1952, he flew F-86Ds, served as squadron and wing maintenance officer in Toule-Rosiers AFB, France and Hahn AFB, Germany, retiring in 1960. Later served as air traffic controller with FAA from 1961-73 in Arizona, Colorado and California, then medically retired. Graduated from Napa College with Real Estate Certificate, passing the State Exam in 1975.

Roland passed away May 9, 2001 and is buried in Dallas-Fort Worth National Cemetery. Survived by his wife, Virginia (Dettman), one son, two daughters and seven grandchildren.

ARTHUR G. WITTERS, born Sept. 22, 1919, Canton, OH. Got his BSBC, University of Florida August 1941 and MS-Arch. Engr., Iowa State University in June 1949. Called to active duty (ROTC) on Sept. 15, 1941.

In 82nd and 101st Abn. Divs. 1942-43; pilot training 1943-44; assigned 392nd FS, 367th FG, 9th AF (9 & 19 TAC October 1944; flew 26 P-38 and 40 P-47 missions.

Of note: bombed von Runsted's HQ (Kesselring in command then) March 1945. Served in USAF through September 1965 and retired as colonel.

He was academic instructor USMA; chief engr. and constr. NEAC; first director of installations, USAFA; squadron commander, Air Evac MATS; Chief Architect HQ USAF; Ass't. Dep. Director of Construction HQ USAF.

His awards are Legion of Merit, DFC, Air Medal w/8 OLCs, AF Commendation Medal w/OLC and two DUBs.

Married Beverley Phaup May 16, 1942 and they have four children, nine grandchildren and three great-grandchildren. Arthur operates a construction consulting firm in Orlando, FL.

JOHN T. WOZER, was sworn into the Aviation Cadet Program on Dec. 7, 1942. After basic training at Miami Beach he was assigned to the Gulf Coast Training Command, Class 44-C for Classification and Flight Training. He was commissioned on March 12,

1944 at Aloe Field, Victoria, TX. Assigned to 1st Air Force for P-47 flight training which included Bradley Field, Suffolk County Air Base and Dover, DE, AFB.

Transferred to pre-combat flight training at Atcham, England. Assigned to 9th AF Combat Operations with 366th FG, 366th FS in November 1944. Completed 45 combat missions from the Battle of the Bulge to the end of the War. Decorated with Air Medal w/8 clusters, Belgian Fourragere and Unit Citation. Discharged in October 1945.

Earned BS degree in aeronautical engineering, Penn State and MS in mechanical engineering, University of Buffalo. He's past-president of 366th FG Assn. Married to wife Winnie since 1955, they have three children and six grandchildren.

MITCHELL R. WRIGHT joined the USAAF May 31, 1943, Mitchell Field. Served with the 926th Avn. Engr. Bn., 8th AF in England and the 834th Avn. Engr. Bn., 9th AF in France. They built the D-Day landing strip   above Omaha Beach and lost six men in the war. Two are in the military cemetery located approximately where they built the landing strip.

Left the 834th in October 1944 and finished the war with *The Stars & Stripes,* the newspaper that was delivered daily to the front.

A unique event in military history, received the Bronze Arrowhead, Normandy Beachhead, Unit Citation 834th Avn. Engr. Bn. Middle Eastern, Service Medal, Victory Medal, French Overlord Medal.

Continued his newspaper career after the war with *The London Daily Mail, The New York Post, The New York Herald Tribune, France Soir* and *Paris Match.* Presently a resident of France and the US.

RICHARD I. WRIGHT, born July 21, 1926, Waterfall, PA. He enlisted in the Air Corps Reserves Feb. 29, 1944 and began active duty Nov. 22, 1945. Assigned to 43rd ADG, 9th AF, Erding, Germany and served as airplane and engine mechanic in the ETO.

His memorable experience was visiting Dachau Concen-   tration Camp. Discharged from regular service Dec. 3, 1946, Separation Center, Fort Dix, NJ in December 1949 from Reserves. His awards include the American Campaign Medal, Army of Occupation Medal, Good Conduct Medal and WWII Victory Medal.

Married Jane Fogal June 20, 1953 and they have two daughters. After 44 years Richard retired from the manufactured housing industry as purchasing agent and sales manager.

Courtesy of Carl F. Heagey.

William Horlacher (Courtesy of Mrs. William Horlacher)

Courtesy of E.F. MacLean.

Thomas A. Williams (Courtesy of Thomas A. Williams)

July 1944, Chalgrove, England. (Courtesy of Clifford R. Fisher)

James L. Fall's identification photo taken by Germans after one month of captivity. (Courtesy of James Fall)

Ted Blair, Germany, WW II. (Courtesy of Theodore Blair)

377th Squadron, 362nd Fighter Group. Pilot-1st Lt. Henry J. Pochily, Crew Chief-Sgt. Russ Ewen, Amorer-"Cookie"? (Courtesy of Henry J. Pochily)

Capt. Howard Curran, 510th Fighter Sqdn., 405th Fighter Group receiving DFC from Gen. Hoyt Vandenburg, CG, 9th Air Force, at Rennes, France, August 1944. (Courtesy of Howard J. Curran)

First View of France, July 1944. (Courtesy of James T. Lee)

Remagen's Ludendorff and Ponton, April 1945. (Courtesy of James T. Lee)

Index

A
Ambrose, Stephen 46
Ammerman, G.R. 50
Anderson, Charles W. 50
Anderson, James M. "Andy," Jr. 50
Andrus, Robert D. 51
Antrim, Joseph C. 51
Aurilio, Lester 42

B
Bachrach, Capt. 43
Baloga, John M. 51
Barr, William T., Jr. 47, 52
Bartley, Roy D. 52
Bealmer, Willis R. "Bill" 52
Beam, Rosenham 12
Bennett, Chuck 31, 32
Bennett, Leonard R. 6, 23, 52
Berchek, Frank 53
Bernson, Carl B. 53
Billings, Archie E. 53
Blair, Theodore R. "Ted" 54, 100
Blondell, Joan 36
Boreck, Chet 54
Bourquin, Henry N. 54
Brereton, Lewis H. 7, 12, 43
Brulle, Albert 32
Brulle, Robert Vanden 31, 32, 55
Bullock, Ken 55

C
Carll, Paul L. 55
Causbie, J. Robert 56
Childs, A. David 56
Cirantineo, Bernard 57
Cline, Richard Austin 57
Cohea, James B. 57
Cone, Richard E. 57
Conner, Wendall 58
Connor, Francis A., Jr. 58
Cowles, Maynard L. 58
Crocker, Harold 6, 23
Crow, John P. "Jim" 33, 58
Cuff, Frank B. 35
Cunningham, William Ross 59
Curran, Howard J. 30, 35, 36, 59, 101

D
Dahlheimer, Harry 60
Dains, Robert L. 60
D'Avila, Ray V. 61
Davis, Stanley J. 61
Derneden, John 41, 42
Derocher, Arthur C. 36, 61
Dontzin, Benjamin J. 61
Downing, Wayne Edward 62

E
Ehrman, J. Frank 62
Eisenhower, Dwight D. 12
Ellinger, Richard P. 44
Emert, Phill G. 63
Engler, Martin 6, 23
Ewen, Russ 101
Exon, Arthur E. 63

F
Fairbanks, Russell 37, 63
Fall, James L. 64, 100
Fast, Paul E. 64
Fehsenfeld, Fred 6, 23
Fisher, Clifford R. 100
Fisher, Donald J. 65
Fisher, Everett "Bill" 65
Flavon, Maj. 46
Flinchum, James 65
Foster, Beulah 37
Foster, Beulah Dunn 41
Foster, Cassandra 41
Foster, Janet 41
Foster, Sally 41
Foster, William B. 37, 38, 39, 40, 41, 42, 65
Fredricks, William A. 66
Freeman, Roger A. 14, 16
Frodyma, Mike 45

G
Gates, Robert W. "Bob" 66
Gaughren, Laurence C. 6, 23, 66
Gentry, Benjamin 43
Gerbracht, George "Paul" 66
Goodlander, Oliver L. 67
Greenfield, Leo 67
Greenfield, William D. 68
Groo, Richard D. 68

H
Halverson, Colonel 7
Hamlin, John F. 25, 27
Hardin, Doug 35
Harris, Kenneth 68
Havener, John K. "Jack" 68
Heagey, Carl F. 98
Herway, Loren W. 28, 69
Hill, John L. 69
Hitler, Adolph 11
Holt, Harold Norman 70
Horlacher, Mrs. William 99
Horlacher, William Gustav 70, 99
Hovde, Lt. 35
Howard, James H 22
Hussein, Saddam 23
Hutto, Bob 35
Hyde, Donald B. 71

I
Ingrisano, Michael N., Jr. 11, 71

J
Johnson, Colonel 34
Johnson, David C. 21
Johnson, George 6, 23
Johnson, Lewis A. 72
Johnson, Lloyd L. 4, 6, 23, 72
Jones, Junius W. 11
Jones, Kathi 23
Jones, Robert H. 43, 72

K
Kellar, Jack J. 47, 73
Keller, Robert W. 73
Kik, Richard 73
Kirkham, Virgil P. 74
Kleinherenbrink, R.J. 41, 42
Knicklebine, Albert H. 74
Kresge, Lt. 35
Kushner, Max 74

L
Lafayette, Forrest R., Jr. 74
Langell, Wallace H. "Sam" 74
Langmaid, Norman E. 75
Laughlin, Joseph L. 75
Law, Dick 38, 40
Lee, James Thomas 30, 47, 76, 102, 103
Lemos, Jack A. 76
Lindsey, Capt. 21
Little, Augustine Patterson, Jr. 76
Lowman, Raymond P. 6, 76

M
MacLean, Edward F. 6, 23, 77, 100
Magee, John Gillespie, Jr. 45
Magoffin, Morton D. 77
Mann, Charles F. "Chuck" 6, 23, 41, 42, 77
Marcan, Captain 43
Maurer Maurer 14
McAllaster, Daniel F. 78
McAuliffe, General 38
McCrillis, John O.C. 43, 78
McDevitt, George V. 78
McKain, Willliam E. 78
McMahon, John K. 79
McNeely, Kenneth F. "Ken" 79
McNeely, Ramona 79
Mears, Colonel 7
Merwin, Harmon T. 80
Mills, Colonel 43
Milow, Arthur R. 80
Mitchell, Paul D. 80
Morris, Raymond W. 81
Moseley, T. Michael 23
Munder, Fred 6, 23

N
Neason, Frank "Pete" 81
Neral, James R. 81

O
Oyster, Duane E. 81

P
Pantoliano, Thomas D. 47, 82
Parker, George W. 43, 82
Parsons, William A. 82
Paskowitz, Harold 83
Pedone, Vito S. 83
Peterson, John 6, 23
Petrosky, Bernard 84
Phinney, Donald G. 85
Pierce, Richard H. 45, 85
Pitkin, Lt. 43
Plummer, William E. "Bill" 85
Pochily, Henry J. 85, 101
Pullis, George 86

R
Ragase, Ralph R. 86
Rambert, Steve 86
Reaves, Eugene D. 87
Reed, Lt. 43
Rhinehart, Nat C. 87
Richards, Bob 87
Richards, Dick 87
Ringger, Frederick W., Jr. 87
Rogal, Harry C. 88
Rommel, General 6, 7
Roosevelt, Franklin D. 11, 36
Rosvold, Marvin J. 6, 23, 88

S
Saari, Clifford R. 38, 39, 88
Saied, Kemal 89
Sallee, Ralph L. 45, 46, 89
Sanders, Randall E. 89
Sidwell, L. Gene 89
Silverbach, Alan M. 90
Smith, Jack E. 91
Sochocki, Casimier V. "Slim" 91
Sorensen, Harry C. 91
Standring, Charles C. 91
Steiner, Isador "Izzy" 92
Stepnitz, Stanley E. 7
Sutcliffe, George L. 92

T
Taylor, Robert 4
Theis, Anna 41, 42
Theis, Oscar E. 92
Thomas, Provost Marshal 43
Thwing, Julian Dwaine 92
Touchstone, Leroy 43
Troolin, P. 46
Turner, Frederick W. "Mike" 93
Twyman, John V. 93

V
Van Cleef, Paul L. 93
Vanderburg, Hoyt S. 13, 101
Von Braun, Wehrner 40

W
Wagasky, George, Jr. 6, 23
Wald, Charles F. 22, 23
Weber, Kenneth H. 94
Wefel, Ralph M. 94
Weiland, Charles M. 94
White, Egbert Barron 95
Whitehead, Walter 43
Whittington, Major 43
Wier, Jack Arnold 95
Wilcox, Kenneth L. 95
Wilkerson, William E. 96
Williams, Dennis G. 96
Williams, Thomas A. 96, 100
Wisdom, Roland L. 97
Witters, Arthur G. 97
Wozer, John T. 97
Wright, Mitchell R. 98
Wright, Richard I. 98

Y
Yarger, John B. 6, 23
Yeager, Chuck 35

Z
Zerega, Lt. 43

www.ingramcontent.com/pod-product-compliance
Lightning Source LLC
Chambersburg PA
CBHW080637230426
43663CB00016B/2902